MW00824185

CURATE

CURATE

INSPIRATION FOR AN INDIVIDUAL HOME

LYNDA GARDENER + ALI HEATH

PHOTOGRAPHY MARNIE HAWSON

MITCHELL BEAZLEY

'I find myself yearning for experiences beyond the everyday, attracted to the pull of new cities, new spaces, new outlooks, new ways of decorating, new thoughts on creating a sense of wellbeing. It is an obsession – a healthy obsession – that burns within. A journey that broadens thinking, creates new connections and nurtures the importance of community, belonging and roots, instilling a sense of peace in the place to which we return: a manifestation of dreams, creativity and curated memories. Home.'

CONTENTS

Room + Board

THE JOURNEY

It seems fitting that the process of curating this book has taken many eventful turns, through the coming together of two creatives with a shared passion for home and styling. Like the best interiors, thoughts and visual concepts have been tweaked and perfected as conversations developed and ideas gained momentum. We hope that *Curate* will act as an inspirational source and encourage you to trust your own eye and create a home that is personal to you.

The idea began with a connection across two continents: me, a journalist and interior stylist in the UK, and Lynda Gardener, an interior stylist and boutique hotelier in Australia. For a long time, I have held Lynda in high esteem as a global tastemaker, renowned for using the unique and decorative to enhance the narrative within her homes and projects. Having started her career at 19 as a secretary for Levis Strauss & Co., she quickly moved into their visual merchandising team before opening Empire, in Melbourne, in the early 1990s. Regarded as one of the world's first concept stores, Empire ran for 24 years and established Lynda internationally as a doyenne of styling. Since her twenties, she has also slowly created a portfolio of special, boutique accommodations, which are a huge part of her story and self-made success.

While interviewing Lynda for international press features, it became clear that we had both dreamed big and had entered the world of interiors unconventionally. Me, through corporate careers in retail, sales, marketing and as new business director for a top creative agency, before going solo as an antiques dealer and moving into interior styling and writing 16 years ago. Our shared tenacity extended to a mutual appreciation of monochrome aesthetics, natural imperfections, an obsessive love of vintage portraits and collections, and an attraction to soulful, often discarded finds: the seed of an idea for this book.

The foundation of *Curate* is home: the one place where we can be our most authentic. The book is not about creating a perfect showcase, or advocating a quick-fix, trend-led look – the opposite in fact. It is about unique, uncontrived spaces that reflect personal needs and life stories, and the slow curation of revered pieces, from different centuries and countries. Imperfections are celebrated, environment is nurtured, and a sense of timeless longevity is enjoyed. It is about raising spaces and objects above the realms of function and surface beauty; to create an unforgettable, lasting aesthetic.

The book features Lynda's seven properties, along with three more homes, including my own, which illustrate how each owner's style has influenced individual environments. The book explores eight elements that, when considered together, can help transform the alchemy of a space: palette, nature, textiles, lighting, old and new, storage, collections and art. As well as these insights, practical ideas are shared, to inspire further. For us, making a home is about being curious and being guided by what makes you tick. Spaces don't need to be big and finds don't need to be expensive, you just have to love them.

Being in tune with each other's interior style and spirit has made the process of bringing to life our creative vision for the book hugely fun and rewarding. We encourage you to see your things in a new light and begin the *Curate* process for yourself. Thank you for sharing our journey. We hope it inspires you to keep evolving yours.

ALI HEATH

Interior Stylist • Hotelier • Curator • Dreamer •
Lifestyle Store Concept Starter • Traveller •
Bauwerk Colour Collaborator • Creative •
Night Owl • Collector • Forager • Storyteller •
Concoctor • Instagram Addict • Animal Lover •

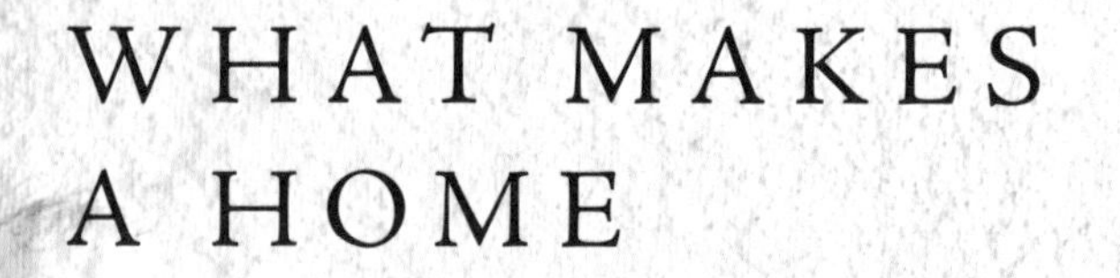

WHAT MAKES A HOME

- **A timeless interior**
  Free from trends, buy once buy well, longevity, things that matter.

- **A feeling, not a place**
  Belonging, safety, curiosity, dreams, nostalgia.

- **A considered palette**
  For us, monochrome meets natural, always with greenery and foraged finds.

- **An individual nest for collections**
  Often simple, basic finds and never about the value.

- **A celebration of history**
  Rich in patina, full of provenance, recycled, repurposed, heirloom.

- **A backdrop for displays**
  An instinctive mix of the right objects and finishing touches.

- **A textural retreat**
  Natural linens, hemp, jute, canvas, wool, cashmere.

- **A mix of raw materials**
  Concrete, wood, stone, marble, glass, steel.

- **An inspiring canvas for artful arrangements**
  Sketches, oils, landscapes and always portraits.

- **A place that is continually edited, curated, layered**
  But never wholeheartedly changed.

- **A look that grows with time**
  And gets better with age.

- **An atmosphere that feels real**
  A true reflection of who you are and what you love.

- **A lived-in haven**
  Where nothing is ever overdecorated.

- **An escape**
  Somewhere to have fun, party, catch up, dream, create, switch off, relax, rejuvenate.

- **A space slightly worn around the edges**
  Pieces left unpainted and broken – it is part of the charm.

- **A curation of old and new**
  Antique, vintage, found, handcrafted, contemporary.

- **A comfortable space where family and friends are welcome**
  A safe haven, full of memories, unique.

Envoi des MINOTERIES de CHAUDENAY S.A.
71 CHAUDENAY (S.-&-L.)
M
Remis le
Portugal
234

WHAT IS AN INTERIOR STYLIST

- **The Curator**
  The seemingly chaotic can be turned into something amazing.

- **The Scanner**
  Notices a bargain or gem a mile off and will scan a room in seconds for just the right thing.

- **The Obsessionist**
  Intrigued by groupings in odd numbers, perfect pairings and unique setups. 'Nearly there' just will not do.

- **The Forager**
  Knows all the best walks, markets, suppliers, neighbours and off-the-beaten-track spots to source the 'right' foliage.

- **The Compulsive Seeker**
  Can never walk past an antique store or flea market without popping in.

- **The Prop Finder**
  A stylist's car is always piled high, just in case. Bags, props, stock – you name it, it's there.

- **The Matchmaker**
  Mixing and matching is their thing. Think antique shops, high street or designer stores. Doesn't need to cost the earth to look fabulous.

- **The Homemaker**
  Ten houses would still not be enough space to express their appreciation of different interior looks fully.

- **The Perfectionist**
  Always notices the wonky mirror, lampshade, picture – sometimes that is just the effect they desire.

- **The Image Hoarder**
  Piles of books and stacked magazines. Flicked through and scrapbooked, they are a constant source of ideas.

- **The Visionary**
  Always curating fresh displays, making the perfectly imperfect bed and planning new home ideas.

ELEMENTS

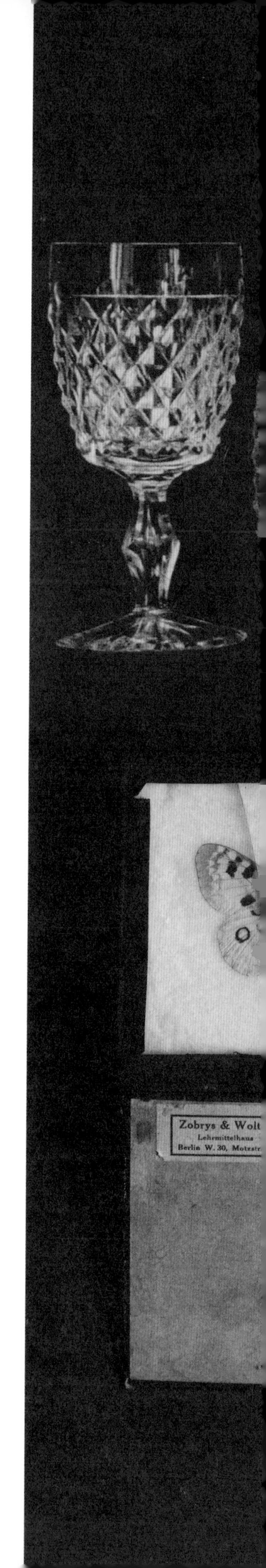

BEAUVAIS. — Lycée Jeanne Hachette.
ND. Phot.
W. PHILLIPS
SOUTHAMPTON
ITALIAN-ENGLISH
ENGLISH-ITALIAN
DICTIONARY
with
Imitated Pronunciation
HUGO
DIZIONARIO
ITALIANO-INGLESE
INGLESE-ITALIANO
con
Pronuncia Figurata

PALETTE

Choosing a colour scheme for your home is hugely personal. It sets the tone for how you live and allows your visual narrative to unfold. Often your wardrobe can be a really strong indicator of what colour preferences appeal, and the idea that people decorate how they dress is usually not far from the truth.

Decisions can be influenced by past experiences and the desire to re-create a look, logged deep in your memory. White or colourful, chintzy or sleek, formal or informal, pared back or bohemian – these triggers can be very powerful and remain with you for life. Simply listen to your head and what makes your heart race: if it sparks joy, the rest will follow.

Ultimately, there are no wrong choices, just what works for you. The trick is to decide on your palette and then stick with it. For many, the decision can seem overwhelming, but within modern rustic spaces things often begin with white, which provides the perfect canvas against which furniture, art and decorative details can take centre stage. There are exceptions to the white rule, but always within a monochrome mix of blacks, chocolate browns, moody greys and calming neutrals.

By sticking to just one palette, decisions become easy and you avoid any temptation to stray outside of those parameters. However, this does not mean white is a safe choice – far from it, in fact. Once textures, patterns, finishes and objects are layered on top, you begin to raise the bar of individual style. White, instead of being about minimalism, can often be the foundation for a maximalist look, full of depth, collections and stories.

Remember, whatever palette you choose, own the decision. Having the confidence to trust your own judgement is the first step toward making a truly individual home: choices made with integrity and heart will remain timeless.

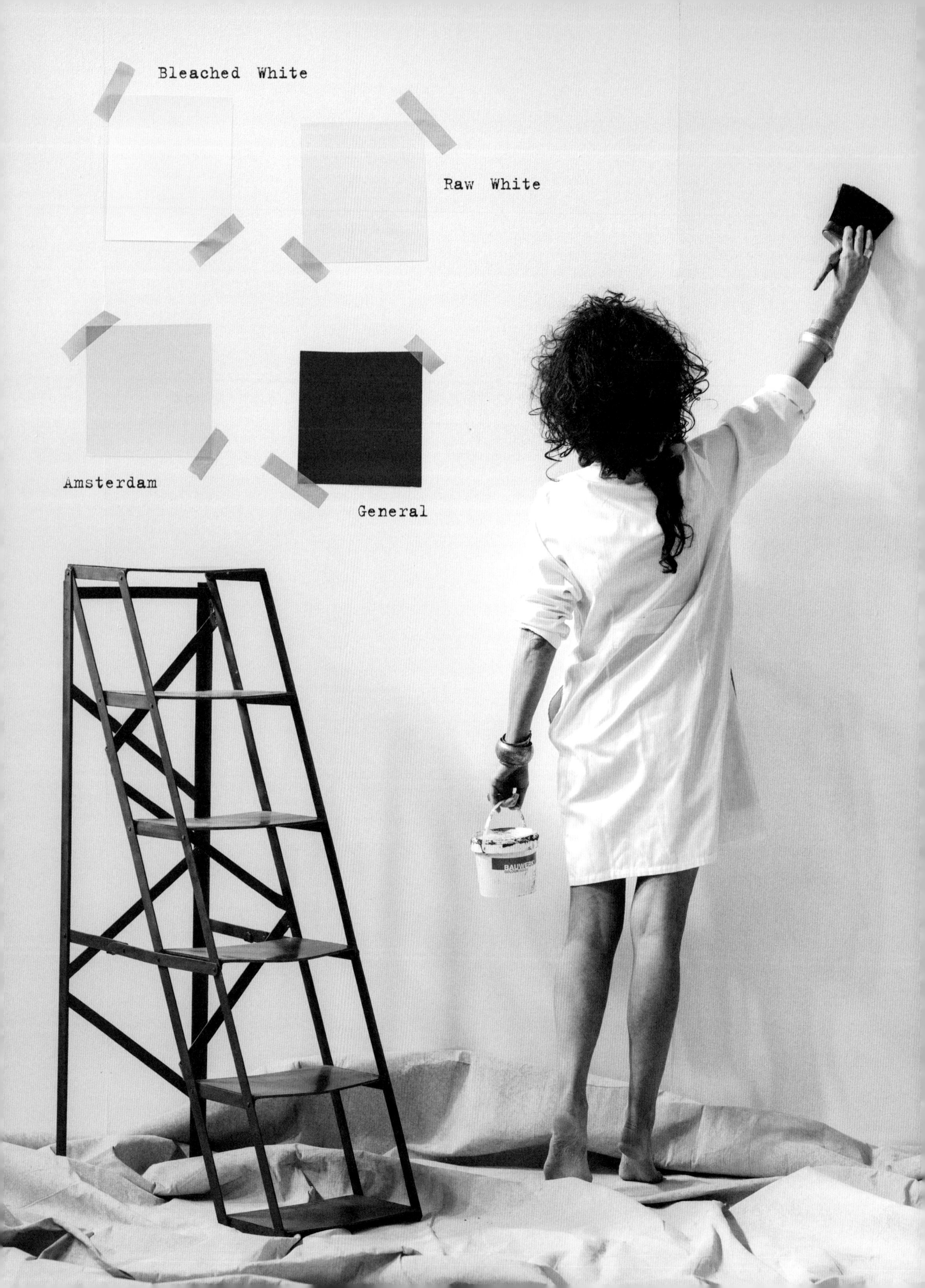
Bleached White
Raw White
Amsterdam
General

PAINT MATTERS
Highly regarded as the 'Queen of White', Lynda has collaborated with the paint company Bauwerk Colour to create a palette of natural white shades that are free from volatile organic compounds (VOC). Complementing these is a coordinating dark army-green shade, called General, named after Trentham General, a café and store created by Lynda in the town of Trentham, Australia.

RURAL RETREAT

The luxurious cast-iron bathtub at Lynda's country home, The Estate, is a lesson in laid-back elegance. Reclamation and salvage yards are valuable sources for similar finds. The timeworn appeal and depth of patina adds a soulful edge that complements the painted, boarded walls.

MONOCHROME CHIC

The artful intensity of monochrome hues lends a sophisticated and timeless feel to spaces. Whether pieces are new, old, handmade, rustic, shiny, timeworn, patina-rich, crumbling or natural, they are united by a common palette and sit harmoniously together, regardless of price, form or function.

WHY MONOCHROME WORKS

- White has a timeless appeal – fresh, practical, restorative and immensely relaxing.
- Natural light bounces freely off white walls, bringing spaces to life. Not all whites are the same – some are too blue, too yellow or too grey – so always test first.
- The same shade of white on woodwork, ceilings and walls creates a seamless flow and an illusion of space.
- Monochrome instils a sense of calm, allowing the eye to rest when rooms are full of visual stimulus.
- When colour is restricted, the look is far from restrictive. Perfect to offset humble, natural materials, textured layers, indigenous foliage and a mix of antique and contemporary furniture.
- With a limited palette, collections stand out and become easy to curate.
- A simple backdrop provides the freedom to move pieces around and to quickly transform looks.
- White and black are not just two shades – they offer a spectrum of earthy tones and, when used for dramatic effect, punctuate spaces with a change of mood.
- Dark hues create unexpected tension and intensity – inky black painted floors juxtaposed with pure white spaces allow antiques to pop; part-painted velvety grey bedroom walls lend a cocooning richness; and rich charcoal shades, used sparingly on doors, cupboards, within libraries and on blackboard kitchen walls, add a sense of drama.
- A simple monochrome palette gets better with time and works perfectly with old and new finds. Faded, chipped and worn – it's all part of the attraction.
- Monochrome palettes are liberating and provide the foundations for building a modern rustic home.

NATURE

Bringing the outside into your home and nurturing a love of nature is healthy, rewarding and addictive. Whether you live in the city, the country or by the coast, getting to know your local streetscapes, rural paths and coastlines can be a ritual that is relaxing and connects you to both the changing seasons and your local communities. With that connection comes a sense of place and belonging, which can lower stress, promote good health and help us appreciate and look after the areas in which we have chosen to create our homes.

As part of the daily practice of getting out and about, our local surroundings become an ever-evolving source of natural pickings that can be foraged and displayed at home. Dropped branches, twigs, feathers, a single flower popping up through a crack in the pavement, a fallen bird's nest or dried seedheads are all everyday gifts that can help to bring our homes to life.

When planning interior projects, it is also key to consider nature from a design perspective. How can we build and develop our spaces in a way that supports our local environments? How can our windows optimize the outlook onto surrounding natural vistas? How can more daylight be channelled into our rooms? How can our gardens be developed and planted to nurture a sense of wellbeing? How can space be created for indoor plants and trees, to improve air quality? Plants have become fashionable, but their benefit to our health is worth so much more than just their visual appeal.

Nature is about a connection, remembering the world we live in, minimizing our footprint and noticing the passing of time. It has a gentle rhythm and is an essential consideration when creating relaxed, timeless spaces.

GARDEN STYLE

Lynda's bespoke glasshouse, at the bottom of her garden at The Barn, is surrounded by silver birch and natural grasses. This contemporary take on a potting shed combines traditional antique garden paraphernalia, alongside modern-day finds and a relaxing daybed. It is the perfect spot for pottering or taking the time just to be.

BRING THE OUTSIDE IN

Natural finds have a pleasing fragility against hardworking surfaces and, throughout a home, they add an organic feel that heightens the air of vitality and wellbeing. Whether freshly cut, planted, dried or foraged, these natural beauties bring sculptural elegance to any interior space.

But these are deeds which should
not pass away
And names that must not wither.
- Byron.

DISPLAYING NATURE'S FINDS

- Use the changing hues of nature to provide seasonal colour at home – sculptural, earthy forms work well within a monochrome palette and add a wealth of texture to a room.

- Consider foraged finds as part of your collections; this immediately places a value on your discoveries and enhances their visual worth and meaning.

- Curate these pieces within your displays – they are part of your story and daily narrative.

- Use decorative vessels to contain your finds: glass domes covering single allium heads; vases packed with dried hydrangeas; dishes brimming with seasonally foraged nuts; jars filled with collected shells; bowls piled high with decorative pine cones; shelves home to pieces of ethically sourced coral and urns overflowing with autumnal ferns. Individually all mini works of art, and displayed throughout the home, they lend a cohesive connection to the outside world.

- Create a nature table – a fallen magnolia branch, placed on a table among candlesticks and propped-up art, creates a wonderful opportunity for a still-life display. Simple, pared back and strikingly elegant.

- Use natural ingredients as aromatic displays – think oversized dishes piled with organic lemons, or zinc pots bursting with fresh herbs.

- Fill bowls with treasured beach finds – pebbles soaked in essential oils or sprayed with your favourite perfume add an earthy organic touch to bathrooms and coffee tables.

- Use your rafters for display – hanging baskets filled with lush green plants not only save space but also lend a tropical feel to your home.

- Bring the outdoors in – plant trees in ceramic planters or vintage dolly tubs and arrange them throughout your home. The effect is grounding and instils a desire to nurture natural finds.

TEXTILES

Textiles conjure emotions of necessity, comfort and luxury. They are an integral part of our daily lives at home and influence every space within it: from upholstering our furniture, dressing our windows and layering our tables, to drying us after a bath and enveloping us within our beds.

Textiles have to work hard in terms of practicality, longevity and unity. Whether tying an interior seamlessly together or creating discourse through contrast, textiles determine how we feel about our spaces. They take many forms – patterned, plain, sleek, colourful, natural, monochrome, textured, antique, new. When choosing fabrics for cushions, bolsters, floor seating and upholstery, consider a mix of textures, patterns and colours, but always within your chosen palette. This will enable you to move pieces between rooms and curate fresh looks throughout your home, while retaining a cohesive overall style.

The level of cosiness can be changed seasonally. In winter, wools, cashmere, felts, furs and knitted throws come to the fore; in summer, cool cottons and sheers are ideal. Whatever the season, linen is always a favourite. Good quality organic bed linen is an investment, and it will remain with you for years, getting softer and more beautiful to use the older it becomes.

Vintage timeworn textiles are often treated as part of a collection – bought first for their visual and textural appeal and considered later for their practical application. Within a modern rustic home, antique finds add a sense of individuality and personality. Think monogrammed linen sheets used for bolsters, tablecloths and bed throws; vintage hemp used for headboards; and old hessian (burlap) grain sacks repurposed as sofa and chair upholstery – timeless hard-wearing textiles that when repurposed in fresh, innovative ways, bring a creative edge to our homes.

EMBRACE THE COSY

Adding layers of throws and cushions creates textural appeal and heightens the welcoming allure of core living areas. Change textiles and creative art displays to reflect seasonal palettes. Thin bracket-free shelves are a wonderful way to display propped-up paintings and sketches.

IT'S A WRAP

Layer, layer, layer. The more tactile spaces become, the more inspirational and welcoming the home. Collect textiles on your travels, from your favourite stores and independent makers. Their comforting and aesthetic appeal adds a unique dimension, and if you choose natural fibres, they will get even better with age.

LAYERING THE PERFECTLY IMPERFECT BED

- Create a more edgy, less formal feel and help turn messy and dishevelled into just-thrown-together cool.

- Work with the best feather quilts, duvets and pillows you can afford – plump and full means inviting and welcoming. We spend a lot of time in our bedrooms, so beds should feel luxurious and retreat-like. This is a place to invest in quality.

- Pure linen works brilliantly – warm in winter, cool in summer. Natural linen fibres look better wrinkled, so no need to stress about ironing. Crinkly adds to the appeal.

- Mix things up – earthy shades of clay, graphite grey, chocolate and dark green add warmth and combine well with lighter tones of white, cream and taupe, for a mix-and-matched look.

- Collect tactile layers – think cashmere throws, woollen blankets, handwoven bedspreads, handstitched heavy quilts and vintage monogrammed sheets. They add comfort and style.

- Begin with a fitted base sheet – plains or ticking stripes are perfect. Build this up by throwing over a flat sheet. Leave more length at the top so you have enough to fold back.

- Add a duvet, in a linen cover of your choice – stylists often add two duvets for extra oomph on shoots. Then fold the flat sheet loosely back over the top of the duvet.

- Dress pillows with linen pillowcases in various shades – pairs of super king, standard and a mix of squares work well. Add them randomly to the bed – on an angle, softly crumpled, positioned for comfort and lounging. Antique linen or hand-dyed velvet bolsters work well, too, as decorative front pillows.

- Leave the flat sheet untucked and gently ripple the duvet to create a lived-in look. Don't think too hard about this – shake it across the width of the bed, sit on it to mess it up and gently tweak it into relaxed folds.

- Layer the top of the bed with loosely draped blankets and cosy textiles. The sum of all the layers is so much more than each individual piece. They can be swapped between bedrooms and will change things up in an instant.

- Want to jump back in? Then your work is done! Remember, it's all about the layers.

LIGHTING

Lighting is often overlooked until the last minute, but it really is vital to plan this at the start of a project or renovation. A key element within every home and each individual space, lighting creates mood and atmosphere and allows you to change the feel of a room throughout the day. Get lighting schemes right and you will elevate your look and possessions, but without consideration, they can make spaces feel flat and dull, and creative corners will go unnoticed.

Within a modern rustic home a mix of old and new lighting works best: think original antique chandeliers and vintage wall lights, mixed with pendants, low-level lamps, industrial desk lights, naked bulbs, metal cage lights and contemporary floor lights. The combination of styles lends a gritty edge to your interiors.

Integrate lights by their timeworn textures: aged brass, rusty metals, scalloped glass, battered enamel and galvanized steel; not to mention more modern-day paper shades, sleek conical ceramics, rustic basketware, contemporary concrete and handcrafted wooden bead designs. The art is balancing just enough of each, so one does not overwhelm or dominate.

Create unique lamp bases using all manner of repurposed urns, wooden carvings and antique ceramic pots. Dressed with handmade lampshades made from vintage linens, they will create a distinctive look within a room.

Remember to consider lighting in both your garden and the entrance to your home. Good lighting is just as important externally, whether welcoming porch lights, repurposed bulkhead lights for courtyard walls, strung fairy lights, or more extravagant lighting schemes that highlight particular areas of furniture or planting.

By illuminating your home thoughtfully, you will bring spaces to life and add comfort to your whole interior.

INDUSTRIAL EDGE
Industrial lighting often appears within Lynda's properties. In The Cottage, a vintage metal pendant and overhead table lamp add a masculine edge to a more feminine scheme. Remember, as your desire to shake rooms up evolves over the years, finds can be moved around the house, from space to space.

LET THERE BE LIGHT
Investing in a few stand-out lights, both old and new, will add drama and the finishing touch to a room. In Lynda's eyes, it is like adding the right jewellery or accessories to an outfit – a vital element that takes time and consideration to get right.

STAFF
ONLY

DRAPING PENDANT LIGHTS WITH STYLE

- As an antidote to expensive electrical changes, use the original ceiling fixture and simply swing the new cord of the pendant light across to a hook, positioned where needed. This avoids creating a new electrical point and offers an affordable and highly creative solution.

- Decide where you want the fixture to hang and the level of light you need: above an island as a statement or for practicality; over an armchair or sofa as a targeted source; within a bathroom as a decorative touch; or adjacent to your bedside as an alternative to a table lamp.

- Choose a flex. There are so many beautiful ones to pick from – everything from round and twisted fabric cord, woven linen and earthy hessian (burlap), to rustic chunky rope, modern see-through or sleek tactile rubber. You can source every texture and colour imaginable.

- Decide on the length of flex, then add one to two metres extra. This will enable you to coil, twist and play with the flex, to create a laissez-faire looped effect. It also means the light can be moved flexibly across different spaces within a room. Always ask a qualified electrician to install lights.

- Choose a ceiling hook – old rusty metal pegs, industrial ceiling fittings, galvanized conduit hooks and antique pulleys work brilliantly to anchor the flex.

- Install dimmer switches – with the help of an electrician. They instantly change the mood and avoid any bright glare.

- Have fun choosing the pendant itself – mix a variety of old and new styles – and consider the height at which it hangs. A low-slung pendant will create impact, while one hung too high will look twee and less artistic.

- Don't drape every light fitting – include some that simply hang straight down. Draped pendants used selectively add the wow, but too many will look contrived.

OLD + NEW

When making furniture choices, it is important to reflect on how you function as a household and what styles attract you. Patina-rich surfaces on older finds juxtapose beautifully with the clean lines of newer pieces and handcrafted items, creating visual interest and a sense of individuality that is hard to replicate. Put simply, new makes the old stand out and vice versa; too much of one makes it feel ordinary.

We all have different practical requirements, habits and needs, based on the stage we are at, so decisions are hugely personal. Choosing the right core pieces will have a direct impact on your quality of life, as they form the foundations of your home and will set the tone for how you and others feel within it. A small, straight-backed sofa is not enticing, whereas an oversized, feather-filled, bespoke sofa will encourage you to relax and hang out. An old dining table that can seat eight or more guests, mixed with contemporary chairs, creates opportunities for lively get-togethers. A table for two will always be just that.

Consider what is important to you – do you already have pieces that can be repurposed or re-covered? Do you take quick showers or are long, relaxing baths your thing? Freestanding antique bathtubs not only look fantastic in modern rustic homes, but are also good for your mental wellbeing, providing the perfect place to switch off and unwind. Do you enjoy cooking or prefer eating out? If the latter, a modern fitted kitchen may not be your number-one priority, but vintage cupboards for your collections of crockery might be. You can still choose to have the best-dressed table, regardless of whether you have made the meal yourself.

Choosing the right pieces is as much about practicality, aesthetics and economics as it is about wellbeing and a sustainable social conscience. By thoughtfully mixing old and new, you learn to: give renewed life to old; buy new things based on lifetime choices, not seasonal trends; and create a home that is truly individual and unexpected.

‘I realized my home was a vast empty canvas,
a place where I could tell my story
and create anything I wanted.’

TIMELESS BEAUTY
The eclectic mix of old and new adds a fresh and unique perspective to your home. It becomes about the appeal of the piece, not the latest trend or fashionable find. Combine different periods and styles to ensure spaces radiate an individual beauty that transcends time.

2

THE ART OF CURATING

- Use only what you love – avoid convention and trends. Safe will never be unique, and fashions will come and go.
- Work out what makes you tick – antique, contemporary or a mix? The combination of all makes for truly individual spaces.
- Decide what colours float your boat – discard the rest and work within that palette.
- Decide if you want to go it alone or collaborate – hiring a designer or stylist is about listening, working together and developing new ways of thinking. Both have to want this or else the collaboration will fail.
- Develop a curious mind – create a mood board of ideas, using pages torn from magazines. Instagram, Pinterest, books, films, travel and the natural world are all great sources of inspiration. Once you start collecting images, you will see your natural style shine out.
- Explore – look within your home and view everything with fresh eyes. Decide what will stay, what can be repurposed or what needs to go. Then plan what key pieces your home still needs.
- One step at a time – finish a room before you move on. It will give you clarity, purpose and the drive to continue. However, if you do find the perfect piece for another room, don't let it go!
- Go outside your comfort zone – stylists are renowned for being great shoppers, as they like to seek out treasures. Go to shops, salvage yards and fairs into which you wouldn't normally venture. It will open a whole new world of possibilities.
- Make sustainable choices a top priority – buy once, buy well and use what you have.
- Remember, stylish does not have to mean expensive – some of the best homes are filled with low-cost, personal treasures. You just need the tenacity to find and experiment.

- Move things around between rooms – it will trigger new ideas and show what good looks like. The introduction of a chair, headboard, mirror, lamp or well-placed piece of art can add the edge.
- Decide where your focal points are for creative display – a mantelpiece, bookshelf, corner table, cupboard or wall.
- Work in odd numbers – and begin displays with no fewer than three items, so they look impactful.
- Make layering your best friend – think throws, cushions, a statement light, stacks of books, glass-fronted cupboards and open kitchen shelves, bursting with a mix of curiosities and functional everyday items.
- Celebrate the beauty of imperfections – aged and worn items add depth, character and provenance.
- Remember the power of scent – candles and room sprays are both evocative and decorative.
- Don't make things too perfect – rooms that are overly prissy will not feel welcoming.
- Add the final touches – a sprig of flowers, urns filled with seasonal foliage, antique cutlery (flatware) in a glass vase, a quirky ceramic and always an element of the unexpected.
- Take photos of your setups and things that spark ideas – they are a great record of looks and will trigger other ideas. Pictures will always be useful, too, for your social media and blogs.
- Remember, making a home takes time – and is never finished. The journey should be considered and always evolve. Edit, switch things up and challenge yourself always to make it better.

57
56
55
105
104
103
180
178
60
59
58
31
108
107
106
182
181
63
62
61
36
35
111
110
109
186
185
66
65
64
114
113
187

STORAGE

An ordered house makes for a happy home – but always in a relaxed way. The first step is to look around your rooms and work out which pieces should be hidden and what you are happy to leave on display. It will help you decide what type of storage is needed for clothes, books, collections and life's necessities.

Consider storage solutions that are both practical and aesthetically beautiful – it will raise the visual energy within your home while taming your clutter. Televisions can be cleverly hidden within old cupboards and mounted onto a pull-out rack.

Don't blow your budget on cheap, quick-fix solutions. If you have set your heart on an old wardrobe, be prepared to hold out for the perfect find, which can take time to discover. Antique pieces date well and hold their value: if you move and they don't fit, they can be easily sold. Do consider newer finds – the market is full of beautiful affordable pieces and artisan designs that juxtapose brilliantly with old items. It is all about the aesthetic and the quality of build.

In homes with narrow staircases, antique knockdown armoires, often from Europe, provide a fantastic solution, as they are designed to be dismantled. Check that standard hangers fit and, if necessary, reconfigure the interior with front-to-back rails or shelves. Tops of wardrobes and cupboards can provide a stylish storage spot for collections of awkwardly sized china, baskets and glassware.

Repurpose vintage finds: think old post-office drawers and metal sports lockers for small items and table linen; industrial medical trolleys for crockery; trunks and chests for old photos and family memorabilia; an old armoire for bedding; and an antique haberdashery table as a cook's island. Within a kitchen, antique cupboards lend themselves to the modern rustic look and avoid costly fitted designs.

Use the architectural features within your home to create storage opportunities. Alcoves by fireplaces are ideal spots for built-in bookcases or wardrobes, while low nooks under the eaves can be great places to stack old apple crates filled with fabrics or books. If your purse allows, it is always lovely to commission a bespoke storage piece for your home. In time, it will become an heirloom, too.

SCALE UP

Adding a unique stand-out piece, such as this antique armoire, to a room will create instant impact and gravitas. Such principal items often become the focus around which the room evolves. Don't be afraid to play with proportions; larger pieces can make a space feel more audacious and increase the sense of volume.

A HOME FOR EVERYTHING

Work out what your storage requirements are for each room, then think outside the box for unconventional solutions that will make your heart sing. Storage is a practical necessity, but pieces do not need to look boring if they are to warrant a sizeable place within your home. Quirky means unique.

14
53
2
15
54
25
55
11
42
21
41

ORGANIZING THE PERFECT LINEN CUPBOARD

- A dedicated linen cupboard is one of life's luxuries – if you have the space, it is a valuable storage asset. Antique armoires and vintage cabinets work best.

- Work out what space your cupboard provides and arrange your sheets and duvet covers by colour and size. Treat your stacks of bedding with care. Fold each piece the same way, to create stylish order.

- Stack pillowcases on top of each bedding set in size order – whether standard, super king or square. It will save you lots of time searching, especially if you like to mix and match. Add bundles of decorative pillowslips next to your bed linen: embroidered, monogrammed, velvet, linen or decorative lace, they look wonderful arranged in artistic piles.

- Consider wrapping each set of bed linen with different coloured linen or velvet ribbons, and attaching a handwritten tag to mark the size. In a busy household, this might be a step too far, but if you have the time, it will ensure that your linen cupboard is ordered for life.

- Reserve a lower shelf for decorative cushions, quilts and throws – pieces that you choose to change seasonally but don't need to access easily on a weekly basis.

- Place cedar-wood balls, scented soaps or sprigs of lavender in between the piles of bedding to keep it fresh.

- Scented rocks are also excellent for linen cupboards – Mad et Len's release a heavenly, evocative scent and are contained in artisanal black-iron tins, which also look beautiful.

- If space allows, store towels in the linen cupboard, too – folded and ordered by colour, as before.

- Hand your textiles down through the family – reminiscent of the traditional trousseau, special pieces that have been collected, preserved and looked after can be passed on to future generations.

OORAY

COLLECTIONS

Collections are the wonderfully diverse layers that add authenticity and soul to your home. These are the pieces that best reflect you, your life, your story and your creative eye. Seeing a space through someone else's lens is intriguing – it opens a window to what makes them tick and is a powerful indicator of taste and personality.

An authentic home takes thought and is something you build up slowly, with each purchase triggered by an emotional connection, not a designer name or passing trend. That is not to say you cannot include designer pieces within your collections – you just have to love them for the right reasons. Often the latest 'must-have' piece is tomorrow's clichéd charity (thrift) shop giveaway, so be discerning. Mixing modern, antique, vintage, repurposed, preloved and store-bought items creates an inspiring creative tension – a look that is individual to just you.

When creating displays of your favourite pieces, consider where you would like to experience them each day. Your 'cabinet of curiosities' does not have to sit behind closed doors, instead think: on open shelves; along a mantelpiece; under a glass-topped coffee table; within a wire-fronted armoire; on a stone dish on your dressing table; atop your favourite table; hanging from a rustic peg rail; or simply piles of treasured books, filling an empty corner. The beauty of being creative and having collections to play with is that you can move them around to your heart's content. Open sightlines do work best, though.

Curate your collections by form, function, palette or just because. Think about introducing an element of whimsy; it can be the piece that finishes the presentation and, after all, humour is everything. Consciously consider a mix of heights within your displays, as it will stop groupings from looking flat and uninspiring. Celebrate the hand of the maker – things made with love add heart to a collection, as does the inclusion of art.

THE ART OF ARRANGEMENT
Effortless collections of gathered finds make beautiful still-life vignettes within Lynda's home, The Warehouse (see also pages 74–89). A selection of summer hats adorns the edge of an old armoire, while stacks of paintings, along with piles of vintage books, add decorative interest throughout the interior.

OBJECTS OF DESIRE
Treasured pieces will stand the test of time, as they are part of your visual storytelling narrative. Move them around, touch them, use them, mix practical with sophisticated and forget conventional display norms. Anything goes. It will heighten the visual intrigue and your sense of joy.

FAVOURITE THINGS large old open spaces. warehouses. glasshouses. period homes. semi-demolished buildings. dilapidated history. european mansions. english manor houses. melbourne supper clubs. city buzz. country weekends. looking up. architecture. old lanes. back streets. redesigned spaces in old buildings. cafés. bars. restaurants. art. galleries. parks. the opera. the ballet. nick cave in concert. live performances. travelling the world. exploring. collecting. flea markets. portraits. forests in autumn. hidden coves. feeling that you could be anywhere in the world. peeling paint. cracks in walls. old patina. worn furniture. flaky surfaces. reminiscing. memories. talking. remembering. crying. laughing. walking. eating out. cocktails. rooms full of people chatting over breakfast. aged photos. black-and-white snaps. family history. friends. people watching. meeting new like-minded people. other stylists. the sound of birds in the trees. the warmth of morning sunshine through the windows. messy beds. faded glamour. vintage wallpapers. antique fabrics. linen. texture. layers. claw-foot bathtubs. vintage tiled floors. autumnal colours. monochrome palette. snow-laden trees. old black-and-white movies. vinyl records. collections. vintage cocktail rings. oversized bangles. love letters. handwritten notes. old papers. something old something new. plants. flowers. i-phone snaps. big glasses. dancing. hand-tailored clothes. dress-up. le labo perfume. foraged sprigs. books. black-and-white magazine covers. surprises. kindness. simplicity. details. life.

BUYING GUIDE FOR ANTIQUE FAIRS + FLEA MARKETS

- Visit antique fairs, flea markets and yard sales – they can be great hunting grounds for adding to your collections. Arrive early and position yourself at the front, ready for opening time. The best pieces go quickly, so timing is key.

- Think practically – a pair of comfortable shoes or trainers will be your best friend, and don't forget a hat, raincoat and gloves for bad weather. Remember to: take a bag to carry small items; pack a tape measure; know your measurements for spaces at home; and bring a torch to seek things out on dark early mornings.

- Scan stalls as you walk past at speed – dithering and stopping to look at things you do not want will waste time. The exact piece you are looking for could be just a few stalls away. If you are set on making serious purchases, friends and family will hold you up, distract you and potentially be drawn to the same things as you. Arrange to meet later.

- Don't pretend to be a dealer if you are not – the dealer will know and will disengage.

- Do bargain – ask what the best price is, know your market and recognize when to walk away. If you can afford it, don't be indecisive: buy quickly so other customers can be served.

- Trust your instinct – if a dealer seems odd or the goods appear to be of suspect quality, move on. Your hunch will generally prove to be correct. Make sure you know what you are looking for. For an expensive purchase, ask the dealer for a receipt that dates the piece; if it is not authentic, the dealer will be less likely to oblige.

- If you fall in love with a piece, go with it – the chances are you will not find another again, so if the cost justifies the reward, then don't miss out.

- Take cash – it always equates to a better price. Or just set up a mobile payment account on your phone for speed. Buy quickly, pay, and then return for the goods once you have finished trawling. Do make a note of the dealer's mobile (cellphone) number, though.

- Consider transport – if you are looking for large items, it might be worth renting a van. Take enough blankets to protect purchases. Ropes or bungee cords are also very useful for securing pieces safely.

- Trends come and go, so trust your own judgement and eye – above all, have fun and enjoy the buzz of the find.

ART

Beginning an art collection is highly personal. It says a lot about what captures you creatively and what catches your eye. It does not need to be expensive, or by a famous artist, it is simply about what appeals. Mixing pieces of different eras and styles gives walls a dynamic feel.

An art collection can take a long time to build – many think of it in terms of saving for a special piece, so are put off from starting small. The reality is you could wait a long time to ever commission a painting for yourself, so enjoy acquiring low-cost items that are readily available. Antique fairs, auctions, flea markets and charity (thrift) shops can be great hunting grounds for vintage artworks or preloved finds.

Think of your collection as singular pieces or as a collective. There is a wonderful elegance to a single framed artwork, hung low and off-centre, surrounded by lots of negative white space; or a large abstract sitting on the floor, leaning against a wall. Equally, busy gallery walls, united by one collective theme, such as male oil portraits, vintage nature prints, herbariums or abstract pairings, can make a great impact.

Consider ripping pages from books, magazines and catalogues. If you love it and can frame it, then you have ready-to-go art. Beauty really is in the eye of the beholder.

Art sellers on the streets of busy international cities or in quiet rural markets often provide a great source of original work. Travel is an excellent way to create an art collection that has personal meaning. Each piece will then always remind you of a time and place.

Take time to consider your framing: as with furniture, a mix of old and new works best. Bulldog clips and pegs can also be cost-effective ways to hang pieces. Remember, the way a piece is framed or hung says as much about your creativity as the actual piece of art.

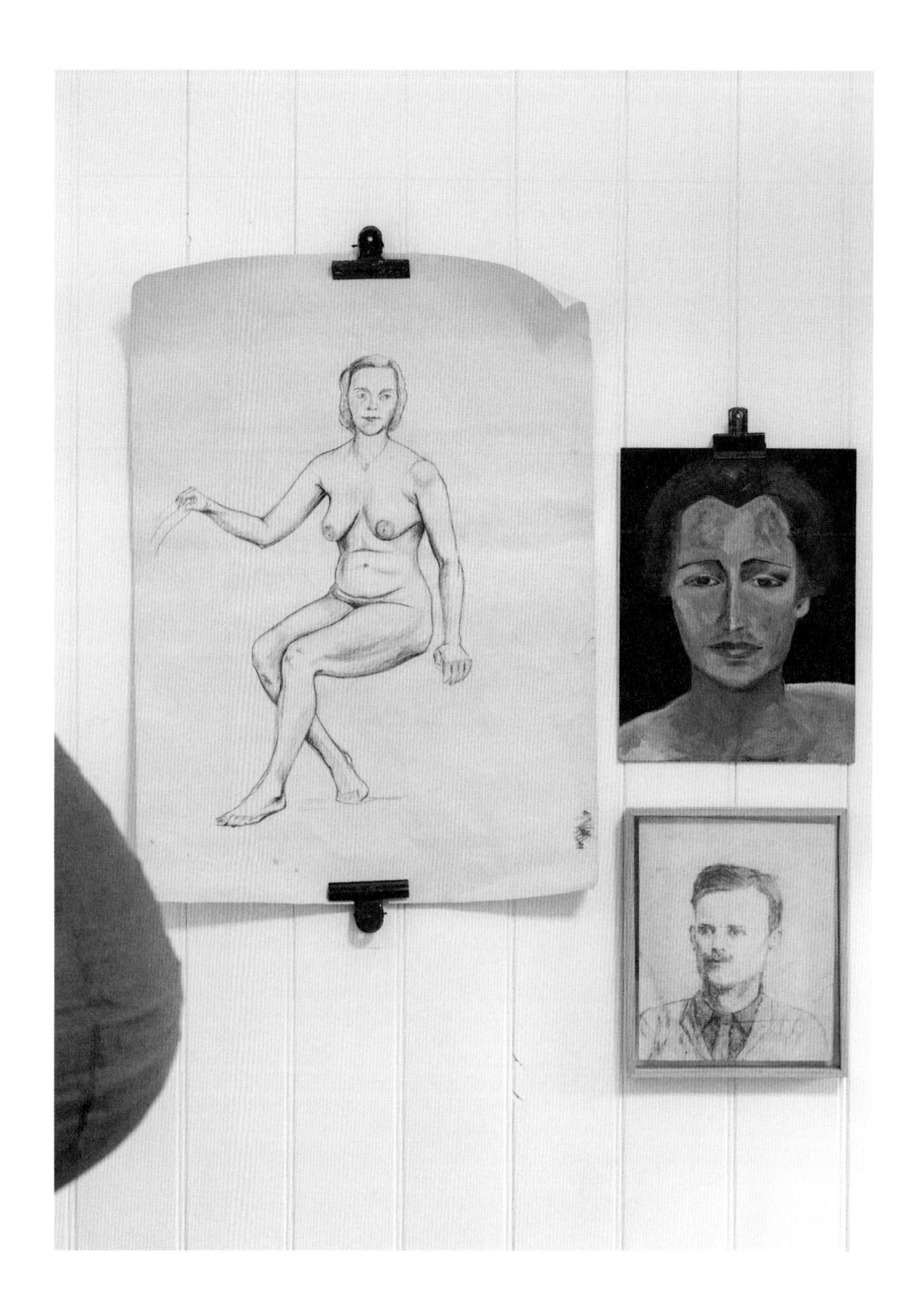

LOVE AT FIRST SIGHT

Sourcing art is immensely individual, so collect only the things you love, then enjoy what you find. Artworks recall snapshots of precious moments in time, so don't tuck them away in drawers – frame them, clip them, prop them and celebrate them.

COLLECT + CURATE

The best art collections comprise an effortless mix of old with new, contemporary with traditional. There is no right or wrong about what you find compelling – choices are instinctive, personal and emotionally charged. The one common factor, though, is that they will add distinctive style to your home.

YOU ARE INVITED TO CELEBRATE
the 50th birthday of
JUSTIN BISHOP
SATURDAY THE 5TH OF OCTOBER 2019
7 O'CLOCK
FOR DINNER IN THE
TEA ROOM
AT THE
Melbourne Supper Club
LEVEL 1/161 SPRING STREET
MELBOURNE
COCKTAIL ATTIRE
KINDLY REPLY BY THE 6TH OF SEPTEMBER
jb50@justinbishop.com.au
Room + Board
Lynda Gardener
1
BAUWERK
COLOUR
BAUWERK
COLOUR
BAUWERK
COLOUR

EMPIRE
MARION
MY FAMILY AND OTHER ANIMALS
UNCLE JOE'S
HUB
GENERAL STORE
& SPARROWS
7
THE
WHITE ROOM
Melbourne
Le Louvre
The Salon

HANGING A CREATIVE GALLERY WALL

- Combine a broad collection of artistic styles and genres – landscapes, naïve sketches, oils, modern art, antique etchings, typographical art, lithographic prints, portraits, pen-and-ink drawings and postcards – all united by your chosen colour palette.

- Decide which pieces you would like to hang and in what arrangement – lay them on the floor and move them around until you are happy with the composition. Put antique frames next to modern ones and always mix the size and style of paintings – large next to small, abstract next to vintage – as it makes for an interesting look.

- Take a snap of the layout you decide on – you will be grateful to have it as a reminder.

- Begin with your largest piece and decide whether to position it centrally or off-centre. That will dictate the flow of the layout. Working outward from this, choose whether to line up your paintings and regulate the gaps between them, or make the gaps and alignments random. The first option will create a more formal look, the latter a more bohemian vibe.

- Decide who will do the picture hanging. For random groupings, you can hang the pieces yourself, as mistakes will show less. If the effect is to look more formal, consider asking a professional picture hanger to make it perfect.

- For large, heavy frames, anchor them firmly to the wall – and always use Rawlplugs (anchors) and screws, which will help an artwork to sit flat.

- For lighter frames, self-adhesive Command strips can be used, without causing any damage to walls. If you are intending for the set to stay for any length of time, however, it is better to use permanent fixings.

- If you are framing a body of coordinating artwork – for example, a set of antique architectural prints – then always choose matching frames and mounts and hang them symmetrically. Nine or twelve matching prints can create a very impactful wall. With a set of antique portraits, leave them unframed – the rawness adds decorative interest.

- Hang groupings from floor to ceiling. If you are hanging a smaller collection centrally, keep it at eye level, and consider hanging a grouping of two to three artworks at a lower level, beside a sofa, as it creates a sense of the unexpected.

ZONING AND PROPORTIONS

- Remember, great design connects people, spaces and objects.

- Plan how you want your spaces to feel – the ambience you are keen to create sets the tone: formal, relaxed, social, private, cosy, minimal, retreat-like or at the heart of everything.

- Make a list of what you need – what areas does the home or open-plan space need to deliver for you?

- Sketch your thoughts on paper and highlight the different zones within a space. Don't forget about storage and animals – knowing where the dog bed will live in a smaller home will save heartache down the line. Use rugs to delineate zones – they can be a great way to break up large areas.

- Consider where the light falls – for a kitchen island or desk, this can be mood-enhancing.

- When deciding on the layout of a room, begin with the largest pieces of furniture – once these pieces are imprinted onto a plan, it will become clear what space you have left.

- Lay blankets on the floor to test scale and proportions – check that you have enough space to walk around furniture comfortably or whether you should consider scaling down or up. The footprints of pieces of furniture are never quite as you imagine.

- Check the visual flow – stand anywhere in the room and ensure your sightline is engaging and unobstructed. Sofas in open-plan rooms work best if they have low backs, unless they are positioned against a wall.

- Remember, balance is key when positioning the remaining furniture within a room. So, too, is negative space. Rooms that are too cluttered can be exhausting.

- Create a 'story' between old and new furniture styles – coordinated looks twee, never unique, so instead unite pieces by palette, texture and shape.

- Aesthetic or comfort? Work out what wins. It will narrow down your choices.

- Consider walkways and flow – do spaces connect, make sense and link logically?

- Stand back and edit – once you have put in everything that is both necessary and decorative. If the space feels too cluttered, keep removing a piece at a time until it feels right.

SPACES

SANTAL 33
100ml 3,4 FL.OZ.
eau de parfum / vaporisateur
natural spray
in MECCA Myer Melbourne
05/08/18
BROTHERS

THE WAREHOUSE

Lynda Gardener

'My look is never about the value, but always about what triggers a visceral reaction: unusual, often simple spaces and finds, which embody a deeper beauty – something I simply could not part with.'

It's a rare thing to enter a home and know instantly that it is a true reflection of the person about whom you are writing. Too many spaces have become absorbed by homogeneous trends and lack that all-important quality of soul. Soul is not something you can buy, it is instinctive: based on personality, individual spirit and a desire to live according to your own rules, surrounded by things that resonate. Authentic homes are full of personal collections, evoking stories of family, friends and precious moments in time.

Lynda's private space is all that and more. Step off the effervescent streets of Fitzroy into her warehouse home, located in the bohemian quarter of Melbourne, and you experience first-hand Lynda's signature style, a look that is layered by a genuine love of the individual and unique. 'The city feeds my soul, but when I come home, it feels like I am entering a secret oasis, tucked away in the heart of all I love, surrounded by all that is important,' she says.

CHARACTER BUILDING

A group of antique male portraits adorns the wall opposite the dining area, on the ground floor of Lynda's warehouse. Sourced in Melbourne and on travels to Paris, Amsterdam and Istanbul, the faces each have a story to tell and form a special part of Lynda's treasured collections.

With floor-to-ceiling glass windows at the front and double-height French doors at the back, leading out to a central courtyard garden, it is easy to see why.

The Warehouse, a derelict former mattress factory, has remained Lynda's private retreat for more than 20 years. Ahead of the curve, she purchased her first warehouse (a disused print factory) in her late twenties and transformed it into an open-plan industrial-style home, at a point when such redundant spaces were of no value. Times changed quickly, and that home would still look as fresh today, if not for the fact that it was snapped up quickly by a keen buyer. From a window of the print factory, Lynda had secretly admired the next-door warehouse: one side all brick and the other adjacent to a single-storey miner's cottage. 'Completely private and not overlooked, it made me hyperventilate the moment I saw it,' laughs Lynda. 'When it came up for sale, it was an opportunity too good to miss.'

Both exciting and dilapidated, the warehouse had been left to deteriorate – brown floors, blue walls, broken windows and no plumbing, not to mention the junk and asbestos. 'I wanted to rejuvenate the spaces, which were split over two levels, and create two simple, open-plan floors that embraced the character of the original brick building.' Downstairs, an inviting dining, living and kitchen level, united by polished concrete floors; while upstairs, an open and tranquil bedroom and bathroom, with a central freestanding claw-foot bathtub, private dressing room and outdoor roof garden, which looks out across Fitzroy's charming old bluestone lanes. 'I painted the original floorboards when I moved in: they are now weathered and chipped, just as I love them.'

Whitewashed walls – all the better, too, for their timeworn appeal – are decorated instinctively: 'I never overthink the design, it's always what feels right. I am not a great cook, so domestic appliances are hidden away, allowing functional spaces to flourish with textures, timeless oversized furniture and decorative details – the glass-fronted cabinet is home to my favourites.' Open one of the antique lockers and discover covetable stashes of tactile French linens, tarnished silver, old crystal glasses and deliciously aged crockery finds. Elsewhere striking metal drawers are filled with all manner of pots, pans and elegant serveware. Nothing is too precious, and everything is used to the max – treasured pieces united by patina, form or palette.'

Throughout, artworks are effortlessly curated: a family of quirky antique male portraits watches over the dining area, and even while we chatted, Lynda sat on the staircase rearranging a collection of naïve sketches discovered on a trip to Amsterdam. 'It takes time to find the right pieces – in fact, I think they find you.' The modern trompe-l'oeil panels, safely brought back from fashion designer Martin Margiela's Paris exhibition, are a perfect example.

'I could never be a minimalist – the draw of beautiful things is a constant joy. Things never need to be expensive, but they must always have a richness that makes your pulse quicken.'

INDIVIDUAL BEAUTY
Low-level comfy sofas, layered with textural cushions, create an inviting spot to relax, framed by an ever-changing collection of artworks, which pay homage to Lynda's travels and creative discoveries over many years. Stacks of books, foraged finds and treasured collectables add intrigue and interest on the handmade coffee table.

HUB OF THE HOME
The simple kitchen with bespoke concrete worktops and stylish open shelves has been created on a budget, but with maximum style. Artfully curated collections of kitchenware, including a treasured selection of American milk glass, sourced over many years, add a sense of understated charm.

OUTSIDE INSIDE
The elegant armoire hides unsightly electrical goods and all manner of practical necessities, while prominent displays of magazines and books are treated like art forms to be enjoyed. Lush plants, trailing greenery and earthy European pots unite the interior with the adjacent courtyard.

Q+A

The Warehouse appeals because?
It's open-plan and light, with large windows onto a lush courtyard – it feels far away from the bustle of the city, yet in the heart of it all.

Your style here is all about?
My life, my collections; feeling content and totally comfortable. Nothing is too precious – it's a home to really live in.

Most successful features?
The open spaces and first-floor bathroom in the bedroom – with a panoramic view of the top floor, surrounded by windows and leafy treetops, it's the most special and private place for a relaxing bath.

Best advice for designing a city warehouse?
Simplicity. It's a warehouse, so don't close it all up, enjoy the freedom around you. Keep big spaces white and bright to let the furniture and collections speak for themselves.

What quality time here means?
Being able to relax and put my feet up, feeling inspired by all my collections and, of course, a long bath at the end of the day.

Paint colour of choice?
Raw White – it's from my collection with Bauwerk Colour.

What's on your walls?
Vintage portraits, oils, sketches, nudes, drawings, butterfly prints and collections; plus hooks and racks filled with coats, bags, rolls of wallpaper and little collections curated over many years.

What's on your bedside table?
Cocktail rings – new and vintage. I'm a huge collector, so they are always near. Plus books and a sprig of green from the garden.

Favourite possession here?
Oh, that's tough – everything! I am very lucky to be the current custodian of an original portrait painting of my great-grandmother, from the late 19th century. Also very special to me are all my parents' love letters from their courting days in the late 1940s.

Best seat in the house?
It always comes back to the bathtub.

What you couldn't live without?
My collections – they are part of who I am and what I do. Looking through new finds and old favourites, and recalling the stories and memories that led me to find them, means everything.

What tunes are playing?
My playlist has a lot of Nick Cave.

What's on the table for dinner?
I'm not much of a cook and am surrounded by the best restaurants and cafés, so I tend to buy delicious food in. Every night is different!

Tell me something no one knows about this home?
When I bought it 20 years ago, the ground floor was full of old cars.

What noises can you hear?
At the front, cars, people chatting and trams whooshing by; further in, it's all birdsong and quiet. I feel alive with all the sounds around me.

Scents evocative of here?
Essential oils – lemongrass is a favourite – and I'm in love with my Le Labo, Santal 33 perfume and wear it daily. The house is infused with this scent – it's me all over.

Favourite season at home?
All seasons! In spring and summer the courtyard and rooftop gardens come alive; in autumn and winter it is still light and warm inside.

This space makes you feel?
At home, safe and happy.

What are you dreaming up next?
It's pretty much exactly as I want it, but I am forever moving around the things I love.

SPLIT LEVEL
The open-plan top-floor layout has a relaxed, bohemian vibe. Lynda is a great believer in designing spaces to meet your individual desires, not anticipated future resale needs or expected norms. Follow your heart, not your head.

PAST + PRESENT
The vintage French bed is framed by an artful grouping of landscapes and portraits, united by their colour palette and intrinsic appeal. The rope-hung pendant light adds rustic elegance to the lived-in interior space, while antique shutters softly diffuse natural daylight from the external cityscape.

IF WALLS COULD TALK
Lynda's walls are lined with endless collections of personal artworks that recall memories of people, places and events. The portrait of her great-grandmother is a much-treasured work that takes centre stage on the wall that leads out to the roof terrace.

The
Thrifty Kitchen

THE ROOM

Lynda Gardener

'I never started out wanting to own so many properties. I am a risktaker, but it has evolved slowly over the past 25 years, with hard work and saved funds.'

Creating something out of nothing is an art form. On a grand scale, with huge budgets, anything is possible; but take a smaller space, with limited funds, and watch many run a mile. For Lynda, that is all part of the challenge and the appeal. Despite having no formal training in architecture, interior design or styling, Lynda is the sum of all these skills, having learned instinctively on projects, by working with a great builder and through a need to make her budgets work hard. 'The only prerequisite to them all is that I had to feel I would want to live there myself.'

For those starting out on the property ladder, these lessons in dreaming big are aspirational and provide many pointers for turning the everyday into something exceptional. The key ingredients behind Lynda's successes, though, are built around a reliance on what she does best: trusting her judgement and intuition. Regardless of job title, she has a creative flair for coaxing the best out of any space, seeing prospects where often none are visible and sourcing creative finds from everywhere, mostly at minimal cost.

PALE + INTERESTING

The stylish all-white kitchen area has layers of tactile interest. Non-traditional storage units, including a medical cabinet, old industrial trolley and bespoke shelf nook, house ever-changing displays. The result is a functional working area that is also creative and visually emotive.

When the canvas has been stripped back to its raw, beautiful state, Lynda perfectly understands how to bring a space to life. The work of a stylist is often not understood, but witness the transformation of a space when a stylist has worked their magic, and observe the power of curation and composition.

The Room is exactly one of those spaces: a disused outdoor toilet block that served Lynda's Fitzroy home, The Warehouse (see page 74), back in its mattress factory heyday. It was derelict, run-down and not fit for purpose, let alone living accommodation, but Lynda saw this as an opportunity. After all, it isn't the square footage that counts. It is all about working with what you have and using all of a property's hidden qualities to create something covetable. In this case, the key is the intimate location, down a cobbled back lane in the heart of Fitzroy, Melbourne, around the corner from the vibrant theatre quarter and historic parks, a ten-minute stroll to some of the coolest restaurants and bars, and a few steps from the city tram.

The space is completely secluded, hidden from view and accessed via a private entrance. One room, yet full of cosy, inspirational nooks, it is a lesson in using every inch of space to create something personal. Think intimate kitchen; a relaxing bed covered in antique linen and a Moroccan wool throw, sourced on travels overseas; a cosy reading corner with a battered leather chair; a whimsically hung pendant, set against an old French armoire; and a small dining table-cum-desk, overlooking a plant-filled courtyard. Only the shower room is tucked behind a closed door for privacy.

'I am at my happiest scouring flea markets for unexpected finds, like the industrial glass-fronted cabinets and old metal trolleys. They allow basic kitchen accessories to work both practically and as creative visual displays,' says Lynda. Around the bed, a collection of random artworks, united by tone, create an inspiring frame. 'I have never bought a painting because of the artist – it is always because of the colour or mood and, more often than not, it's second-hand. When I spot the right piece, I get very animated – not great for my bartering skills, but the reaction tells me it is right. Purchases are always from the heart, never about practical necessity. I guess that is why each of my places is always so personal to me. It's important and how I like it,' she says.

FLEXIBLE LIVING
The study area next to the kitchen doubles as a breakfast and dining space. With views out to the private courtyard beyond, it has a lush feel that is brought to life with books, collected ephemera and seasonal greenery. Painted brickwork and enamelled lighting fixtures enhance the industrial feel.

ALL FOR ONE
The small space is punctuated with oversized finds, which increase the sense of grandeur within the bijou space. Stacks of books, a generously layered bed, a stylish armoire and a welcoming leather chair create a restful and robust interior, with many inspirational and impromptu creative displays.

THE BREAD CARTERS' INDUSTRIAL FEDERATION OF AUSTRALIA
Victorian Branch
Picnic Committee
PRESENTED TO MR W.W. MAYNARD

The
Thrifty Kitchen

The Room appeals because?
It's cosy and unique, hidden in the back of a city street down a bluestone brick path. Opening the door to discover this space is always magical.

Your style here is all about?
Collected vintage finds.

Most successful features?
The room is tiny, but it has everything you need, with three sets of French doors leading out to a little courtyard garden. It is filled with light and sun and has such a happy vibe.

Best advice for designing a city bolthole?
Think about your style and stick to one simple theme.

What quality time here means?
A mini escape – where you instantly feel rested.

Paint colour of choice?
Raw White, from my collection with Bauwerk Colour.

What's on your walls?
There's a gallery wall of battered frames, holding an assortment of old photographs and sketches; chipped antique mirrors and Paris flea-market finds.

What's on your bedside table?
A vintage light, books and foliage.

Favourite possession here?
The dark grey armoire, home to all the things I love to hide, such as the TV.

Best seat in the house?
The worn leather chair, covered in repair patches. It allows you to sink right in and view the entire room in comfort.

What you couldn't live without?
The French doors leading out to the garden. For such a tiny space, they are everything.

What tunes are playing?
Nouvelle Vague and Carla Bruni.

What's on the table for dinner?
Delicious, healthy takeaways from the local restaurants. There are no kitchen appliances here, so it forces you to go out and find something special.

Tell me something no one knows about this home?
Not one piece is left from the building's factory days. Stripped out and renovated, the space has been given a new lease of life.

What noises can you hear?
Birds and yet more birds – it is a real haven.

Scents evocative of here?
Fresh linen sheets.

Favourite season at home?
Spring, autumn and winter – the sun streams in all afternoon.

This space makes you feel?
Cosy and so very comfortable.

What are you dreaming up next?
This space is so right – there's no need to change it for a long while.

THE APARTMENT

Lynda Gardener

'The authentic patina-rich wall surrounding the kitchen window adds soul and provenance. It frames an ancient palm tree spanning the height of the Art Deco building.'

'St Kilda, a vibrant suburb within Melbourne, has a cool boho vibe – loved by travellers and those attracted to city beachside living. There is a great sense of community and connection; and an edgy rawness to the area that, back in my twenties, really appealed and still does today,' says Lynda.

Situated within a refined 1920s Art Deco building, the apartment is at the back of the site, set amid a private courtyard garden that offers a rare, peaceful retreat as you walk in off the bustling streets that surround it. The Apartment is accessed through graceful Art Deco arches that open onto the main staircase which leads up to the third floor. As is typical in buildings of this age, the apartment enjoys high ceilings and wide corridors, creating an extraordinary sense of space for an inner-city escape. 'I have always loved the era and fell in love instantly with the architecture. The proportions and sense of grandeur are very imposing and hard to miss as you drive up to the property,' she says.

The one-bedroom apartment was bought by Lynda more than 20 years ago, during her days with Levi Strauss & Co. Working hard, she wanted to

BASIC INSTINCT

Original patina-rich walls add a utilitarian feel to the kitchen that looks out across a vast tropical palm. Throughout an abundance of greenery adds to the sense of understated lushness and original features are celebrated for their Art Deco appeal.

create a nest egg with a small selection of homes – initially intended as long-term rentals. In 2015, the opportunity arose to take back the apartment and include it within her much-admired collection of boutique accommodation. And with that decision came the time for an update of the interior.

'With the refurbishment, changes were simply cosmetic,' says Lynda. 'The bones are beautiful, and I was so lucky to have the original tiled floors in both the kitchen and the bathroom. They are part of the history here, along with the original plaster walls in the kitchen.'

Throughout, the walls, floors and ceilings have been whitewashed, replacing the original terracotta and black hues. 'When I first bought the place, I didn't have the budget to change the colour schemes, so it felt good to see the space come alive with white – fresh, bright and calming.' Replacement cupboard doors were made for the kitchen units, incorporating the original handles, while simple bespoke shutters were made for all the windows.

Spaces are layered with natural rugs, macramé light shades, cotton throws and bohemian cushions to add warmth and textural appeal. A mix of reclaimed chairs, a contemporary deep sofa and clean-lined storage cabinets is juxtaposed with a raw wood coffee table, humble benches and rustic stools. 'Having these characterful pieces around makes a home feel inviting and informal. A place you can be yourself and unwind in,' Lynda explains.

The monochrome space is filled with a mix of art, including contemporary photographic pieces that lend a more urban, modern-day feel. 'The black-and-white leg shot in the bedroom is a favourite and was bought from a creative local girl, who used to visit my store regularly.' None of the art cost the earth, but its ability to bring walls to life with simplicity and style is second to none. 'Making a home takes time and energy, but the search for unique pieces is always worth the wait,' promises Lynda.

Greenery, used in abundance, adds a natural softness to a space and enhances the sense of bringing the outdoors in. 'This charming retreat in the heart of the city is very special to me. With the shutters flung open, sitting out on the balcony surrounded by breezy tropical trees, you really could be anywhere in the world,' she says.

ROUGH WITH THE SMOOTH
The sleek finish of the gas-burning stove, clean-lined modern furniture and contemporary chandelier contrast with the rustic textures of the footstool, rugs and natural textiles. Abstract and traditional artworks are juxtaposed with stylish aplomb, and decorative objects create a sense of personality within the whitewashed space.

PLANT LIFE
Lynda has cleverly zoned areas to make space for relaxation, work, entertaining and storage. Contemporary baskets, stripy woven textiles and antique glass bottles create informal display vessels for foliage and plants. The pop of bright green punctuates the streamlined, monochrome apartment.

Tim Winton The Riders
TIM WINTON
THE TURNING

The Apartment appeals because?
The Art Deco architecture has so much character – it captures my attention on every visit.

Your style here is all about?
White, light and contemporary, mixed with vintage finds.

Most successful features?
The wide hallway with internal glass doors. It now feels incredibly spacious, and the mass of green plants gives it such a great energy.

Best advice for designing a city apartment?
Keep things light if the space is small – it will create a seamless flow from the moment you walk in. I chose lots of low pieces of furniture for this home, which enhances the illusion of wall height and volume.

What quality time here means?
It's beachside, so it's a space I love in summer. You can walk to the beach, enjoy an ice cream and admire the beautiful old architecture that surrounds you.

Paint colour of choice?
White – a shade called Freesia, by Wattyl.

What's on your walls?
Old and new art, original textures, shelves of portraits and landscapes; and large contemporary abstracts casually propped up on the floor.

What's on your bedside table?
A reading light, a collection of driftwood in a bowl, a small carved African head and piles of magazines.

Favourite possession here?
Besides the art, I would choose the couch, for its unstructured look and style – you just want to jump and lie on it immediately.

Best seat in the house?
The chairs around the table in the sitting room overlook the very beautiful, 100-year-old communal gardens and a huge old palm tree that leans across. It feels as if you are in a treehouse.

What you couldn't live without?
The view.

What tunes are playing?
A mix of Cat Power and indie rock band Sparklehorse.

What's on the table for dinner?
You have a full kitchen here. However, as you might have guessed, I am not a huge fan of cooking, so for me, part of the adventure is to hunt down something simple for dinner, from the local bakery or café.

Tell me something no one knows about this home?
I have never lived for any length of time in this place – always wanted to, but never have.

What noises can you hear?
Birds and soft city sounds in the background.

Scents evocative of here?
Freshness, plants and soil.

Favourite season at home?
It's cosy, whatever the season.

This space makes you feel?
Happy!

What are you dreaming up next?
It has recently been renovated so is in its element right now.

SIMPLICITY + STYLE
The original Art Deco floor is matched with simple ceramic tiles on the bath panel and walls, to unite the monochrome scheme. Black decorative textiles add a moody anchor within both the bathroom and bedroom schemes, and the crocheted pendant light and rug bring a contemporary twist to the pared-back space.

THE STUDIO

Lynda Gardener

'Small, more affordable spaces can pack just as much punch and provide the opportunity for you to break out and discover your freedom. You just need to think creatively.'

Home is the place where you establish roots, carve out the essence of what makes you tick, decide how you want to live and showcase the memories, collections and possessions that matter to you most. The idea of starting out on your own can be daunting and, for many, financially prohibitive. No matter how small your budget, or how compact your space, bijou does not mean second-rate – far from it.

'I bought this simple studio in my early twenties. It was my first investment property and I knew that it would always be interesting as a start-out home. It just needed approaching creatively to make the space work.' What began life as a rental soon became one of Lynda's boutique accommodation stays until, recently, she let it go: 'To someone who fell in love with it and wanted to make it their home,' smiles Lynda.

Situated in an inner-city area of Melbourne, in the heart of beachside St Kilda, the ground-floor studio is one of four located within a 1950s building. 'Fortuitously, The Studio, a single room with a private bathroom,

UNIQUE TOUCHES

The fold-down bed reveals striking textural bedding in soft shades of off-white, pale grey and charcoal. The mirrored panel enhances a sense of space, and The Studio is an inspirational example of how amazing bijou spaces can be, when the design is well considered.

VISUAL APPEAL
Within a very small space, a layered mix of textiles, rugs, low-level furniture and lighting, hung at varying lengths, tricks the eye and senses into imagining a much larger space. Wall-to-wall white surfaces increase the level of light and add to the holistic, simple feel.

came with a large, beautiful side garden and a north-facing aspect. Leafy and cool, it felt like a natural extension of the studio,' observes Lynda.

'The original dark floorboards were immediately whitewashed, to optimize the light and space. White is instantly gratifying, and you could see the space unfurl, as every surface became light,' she explains. To the left of the room, mirrored cupboard doors reflect an all-year-round canopy of green plants and lush garden containers, which double the illusion of flow. The pièce de résistance, however, is the reveal of a hidden fold-down bed. 'Within small rooms, it is life-changing and means that the area can be enjoyed fully as a core living space, without the need to trip over a bed, or compromise on proportions.' Abundant storage also ensures that clutter and the paraphernalia of life are easily stored away. Clever zoning and layering introduce scale and visual interest. The eye is diverted from the tight proportions and instead dances over the array of interesting textures and furnishings that abound: beautiful heavy wool rugs and sisal pouffes; cosy textiles and cushions; and a low-level slubby linen sofa and worn leather safari chairs, which make you want to sink in and relax. 'I always like to combine a few oversized pieces, such as the low-hung crocheted light fitting; it adds a sense of drama to a space,' says Lynda.

'Designing and curating spaces is, to me, all about making people feel instantly welcome and at home,' she explains. Part of that success is due to the mix of old and new pieces. 'I have collected since I was a teenager and The Studio is home to finds discovered over many years at flea markets and antique stores. When I first started out, it was impossible to find newer pieces with a more eclectic feel. Now that choice is so much broader, I love to include select finds, such as artisanal rugs, modern lighting and newer pieces of furniture,' she says.

The mix of styles and finishes adds depth to a look – you don't need to buy expensive items. 'I have never built any homes around the purchase of costly designer pieces,' says Lynda. 'My looks are affordable, relatable and always timeless: good taste does not equate to having to spend large sums of money, it is about buying well, instinctively and having fun in the process.'

The Studio appeals because?
It is the tiniest space, but it was the biggest challenge to decorate simply.

Your style here is all about?
Bright light, white and simplicity.

Most successful features?
The fact that it is one open space, with large windows facing north that let in lots of natural light.

Best advice for designing a city studio?
Keep it simple. As always, make sure that when you walk in the door, the space feels calm and has an instant sense of style.

What quality time here means?
Going for walks by the beach, catching up on my favourite interior books and having quality thinking time – it is a true city escape.

Paint colour of choice?
White, white, white.

What's on your walls?
Naïve sketches hung simply with masking tape.

What's on your bedside table?
Not a lot, as the bed folds into the wall. When sleeping here, I use the wood side table to hold a glass of water.

Favourite possession here?
The Moroccan rug.

Best seat in the house?
The couch, as it offers a view through the windows looking out onto the lush garden.

What you couldn't live without?
The floor-to-ceiling windows and French doors opening onto the courtyard garden.

What tunes are playing?
Chet Faker and Beach House.

What's on the table for dinner?
Same little story – I'm a big fan of local food and eating out.

Tell me something no one knows about this home?
It was my first investment property, purchased with my partner at the time, when I was 24 years old.

What noises can you hear?
Lots of street sounds, people chatting, cars and city life.

Scents evocative of here?
Essential oils, with fresh rosemary from the mini garden.

Favourite season at home?
All seasons – it is super-cocooning in the winter and full of sunlight throughout the whole year.

This city space makes you feel?
Cosy.

What are you dreaming up next?
It has just sold, so no more imagining here!

NEW HEIGHTS
Floor-to-ceiling cupboards and full-height garden doors change the feel of the space, drawing the eye upward and helping to disguise the overall compact proportions. The introduction of abundant seating areas creates distinct zones and a sense of luxury within a more budget-conscious accommodation.

THE BARN

Lynda Gardener

'Creating unique stories is what I love. A space begins, ends and evolves always with my collections: old, new, heirloom – I am a magpie at heart.'

'Projects form in my head before they are even a reality, with items stored away ready for the promise of a new venture and just the right spot.' With The Barn, Lynda's latest home project, built in 2019, it began with the purchase of a tiny driveway. This sparked the idea for a simple A-frame structure, which connects a sliver of land from front to back with matching stable doors, mirroring the vista, at either end of the new-build design. This seamless flow creates a sense of continuity and allows spaces within the open-plan layout to work together from every angle. 'Small homes have to work harder, but they make you think outside the box,' she says.

From the exterior, the dark grey, wood-clad home looks functional and contemporary, surrounded by elegant silver birch trees, on a quiet road in Daylesford, Australia's famous spa town, an hour and a half's drive from Melbourne. Step inside, though, and the alchemy is altogether unexpected: simple it may be, but basic it is not. 'The process of designing is never planned or formulaic. It's about closing my eyes and imagining the spaces in my mind

SOMETHING FROM NOTHING

Lynda transformed a redundant strip of land into a stunning one-bedroom, open-plan, vaulted retreat that exudes style, comfort and a sense of calm. Natural textures and sustainable materials – concrete, wood and linen – add layers of interest to the simple barn aesthetic.

– always instinctive and from the heart. I loved the notion of a basic structure opening to reveal a space layered with reclaimed finds, natural textures and treasures that have personal meaning. The element of surprise is everything,' Lynda points out.

'With so much overconsumption, I have always repurposed timeworn pieces: the old school windows, running down one side of the double-height pitched structure, are really at home here – as if it has always been that way. The Barn is where I slow down and relax. As I drive out of the city, I swap the crazy buzz of city life for the draw of the country and a more soporific pace. It has become the embodiment of wellness, a place to just be – on my own, with a friend, or as a boutique rental stay for two.'

The structure went up within nine months and, working with a local builder, Lynda was able to piece together the inspired internal layout intuitively. As you enter, you are greeted by the visually stimulating kitchen, dining and living area: one open-plan space at the heart of the house. Lofty, airy and welcoming, it is the ultimate in escapism and comfort. A long, wide passageway extends on the left, down to a textural bedroom at the back, with low-slung pendants and earthy organic sheets; the central bathroom pod is the only private area. With the ceiling open to the rafters and copious trailing greenery, it feels like an indulgent spa retreat, at one with the outdoors.

Ubiquitous whitewashed walls – the de rigueur colour of choice – are offset with soft greys and warm tobacco hues, which lend a contemporary edge. Raw, organic-feeling surfaces, in concrete and wood, are paired with stylish open shelves and utilitarian peg rails, which create immense opportunities for storage and display. 'I cannot pass a flea market or antique store without succumbing. I am a collector – some would say hoarder – who loves nothing more than curating a home. It's what I do, what makes me tick. The Barn is full of personal pieces collected over many years – butterfly taxidermy from Paris, artworks from years of travels, decorative finds from a nearby junk store and dried flowers foraged on local walks. These perfectly imperfect things are part of my story, and the context and reason for their selection is never lost,' Lynda explains.

Outside the barn, the view is just as unique: a vintage bathtub on the back deck, which steps down through a labyrinth of scented planting to a stylish glasshouse-meets-potting shed, complete with day bed. 'For me, design should always be about how you want to live. If you listen to your own voice and don't follow expected norms, you will create something truly special and individual.'

OUTDOOR LIFE
A matching pair of oversized stable doors at either end of The Barn are united by a run of antique glass windows and encourage a link to the garden and country surroundings beyond. The external lushness is mirrored internally with copious greenery and natural foraged finds.

salus.

DECORATIVE EDGE
In the kitchen, open shelves, a chunky concrete sink and rustic work surfaces are teamed with a contemporary Smeg refrigerator and abundant decorative touches. The modern circular table doubles as an area for entertaining and a display space for favourite finds, including the white plaster bust, sculptural branches and locally gathered flowers.

UTILITY CHIC

Contemporary peg rails create valuable storage space for a collection of practical, yet beautiful, household brushes. Wonky baskets and woven pendant lights add warmth and textural interest, alongside collected ceramics, naïve sketches and linen textiles in earthy hues.

The Barn appeals because?
It's contemporary with a twist.

Your style here is all about?
Open-plan layout, high ceilings, huge barn doors and oversized windows – it feels like a large glasshouse with plants filling its core.

Most successful features?
The pitched height of the ceilings and the salvage-yard finds – the vast, old schoolhouse windows make the place feel unique.

Best advice for designing a new-build country barn?
Stay calm and breathe – lots may go wrong and you may be totally tested on all levels, but the outcome will be worth it.

What quality time here means?
I always draw breath when I walk in through the large barn doors – it is an escape like no other and takes you away to another place. I read, sprawl all over the moveable couches and sleep the best sleep imaginable.

Paint colour of choice?
Bleached White, from my collection with Bauwerk Colour.

What's on your walls?
Shelves filled with old and new collections – vases, trinkets, old butterfly boards, pottery, crockery and many plants; lots of handmade hooks to hold bags, baskets, brooms and tools; sketches from my last trip overseas; and portraits collected from near and far.

What's on your bedside table?
Dried flowers in a vase, a bowl and a few books.

Favourite possession here?
My thriving plants – every visit they seem to have grown larger and larger, which makes me so happy.

Best seat in the house?
The moveable centre couch – it's THE spot from which to view everything– and the day bed in the glasshouse-cum-potting shed. This extra building was a total extravagance but added another dimension, which I love.

What you couldn't live without?
The windows and the high ceilings – oh, and the plants.

What tunes are playing?
Early Johnny Cash, Bob Dylan and Neil Young.

What's on the table for dinner?
Dare I say it again? Dinner out!

Tell me something no one knows about this home?
It literally took blood, sweat and tears to get this finished and nearly broke me, but I got there and am so very proud of it all.

What noises can you hear?
Lots of birds singing in the large trees surrounding the property – it's in the country, so there are so many exotic varieties.

Scents evocative of here?
Fresh linen, fresh paint and fresh air.

Favourite season at home?
All seasons.

This space makes you feel?
Special, alive and like jumping for joy – creating it from scratch was such a personal accomplishment.

What are you dreaming up next?
It's brand new, so not a thing – well, apart from adding to my ever-growing collections!

SIGNATURE STYLE

The low-level bed offsets the imposing loftiness of the barn. Symmetrical pendant lights in earthy tones are complemented by the warm hues of leather, wood and abundant textiles that enrich the cosseted feel. Randomly hung sketches and paintings enhance the laid-back vibe.

MIX IT UP
The concrete sink and contemporary black taps (faucets) combine with industrial mirrors, a clean-lined towel rail and rustic benches. Open to the rafters, the central bathroom pod exudes understated cool and continues the feeling of being at one with nature.

AWAY FROM IT ALL
Lynda regularly escapes the fast pace of city life for the slower rhythm of The Barn. The classic 1965 blue Mercedes, a 230SL Pagoda convertible, is Lynda's pride and joy and the perfect vehicle to enjoy the country drive, often stopping to look out across Wombat Hill to Daylesford below.

AGAVE
FILIFERA

THE ESTATE

Lynda Gardener

'Relaxing in the roll-top bathtub with the French doors ajar, listening to the birds and catching the warm scent of rosemary and sage, is just the best.'

'I was immediately enchanted with this property, from the moment I drove up. I am a serial renovator and flicking through the property pages is an addiction of mine. Since buying The Cottage (see page 152) in nearby Daylesford, this area had appealed and I would often take a detour, on the tree-lined country drive from Melbourne, to stop at Trentham, the picturesque town where The Estate is located. Trentham has a great community spirit and one main street with a strip of old-fashioned shopfronts, including a bakery, a bank and two fabulous pubs. It is so gorgeous that I set up a beautiful café and store here in 2017 – The Trentham General – where work on my collaborative paint range with Bauwerk Colour also began...but that is another story.'

'The Estate, home to a three-bedroom Federation-style cottage, came with outbuildings and the most incredible 1-acre [0.4-hectare] plot – to say it is mesmerizing is an understatement.' Think fruit and herb plants, abundant orchards and a kitchen garden that keeps guests satiated with supplies: broad beans, Swiss chard, broccolini, kale, radishes, beetroots, leeks, garlic, spring

ROOM WITH A VIEW
The sitting room, with its whitewashed walls and textural surfaces, has a calming ambience. Beautiful reclaimed French doors connect the space to the garden, while the handmade wooden coffee table and stool enhance the natural feel.

onions (scallions) and so much more. 'I have a lacklustre approach to cooking, but when I stay here, I always have a pot of vegetable soup on the stove; or a huge bowl of freshly picked salad. There is something very romantic about growing and consuming your own produce.'

The main house, built in 1902, is clad in the original wood and has a wraparound veranda with panoramic views of the garden. With just one neighbour, the space enjoys complete privacy. In warmer months, doors are flung open wide and the breeze from the trees filters through the house. In cooler inclement months, the house takes on a cosy appeal: fires are lit, shutters are pulled, and deep sofas and battered hessian (burlap) and corduroy club chairs offer an enveloping embrace. 'The space is about enjoying the simple pleasures and taking some time to kick back and unwind.'

'There is a wonderful soul here: everything is slightly off-kilter, with original floors, windows and doors adding a sense of provenance.' The structural bones were sound – a warren of simple rooms, flowing around the one-level building – but throughout, Lynda has worked her magic on reviving the interior. An elegant new bathroom was added, and the kitchen was redesigned in a deconstructed, traditional-meets-contemporary style, with bespoke cast-concrete work surfaces and floors, and open shelves displaying a burgeoning collection of ceramics and china. Fireplace surrounds were recast in concrete too, and the modern aesthetic juxtaposes perfectly with the historical origins.

Throughout, a monochrome palette plays out: simple whitewashed spaces punctuated by dark-stained floorboards, occasional soft-grey walls and sculptural earthy foliage. Abundant textiles and rugs, in shades of off-white, oatmeal, brown and black, add tactile appeal, while natural linen bedding ensures the two bedrooms feel indulgent and welcoming. An oversized landscape wallpaper panel creates a sense of drama as you enter the house, via the dining room, and is thoughtfully mixed with an inspiring collection of landscapes, still lifes, pen-and-ink sketches and portraits. The portly gentleman above the fireplace is a particular favourite of Lynda's. Timeworn and personal, the house curates a strong narrative from prolific years of sourcing – with many pieces collected during Lynda's late teens. 'I can't bear to part with things and love that guests get as much enjoyment from them as I do.'

Outside, an old potato picker's shed has been creatively transformed into a vaulted third-bedroom retreat, with the original cast-iron tub from the main house adding an unexpected sense of luxury. The barn, one of the main attractions when Lynda first viewed the property, has been converted from a run-down shed into a stylish event space – extended, reclad and insulated, but with the raw modern–rustic aesthetic preserved. 'The barn is now used for weddings, workshops and other gatherings; it is a beautiful space that can be dressed up or kept pure. I love that the house and barn are being enjoyed by others too. The spaces were bought within a few hours of having seen the advertisement – faster than choosing a new pair of shoes, but now very much old worn-in favourites.'

RUSTIC RENOVATION
Dark floorboards and bespoke concrete fireplaces are combined with earth-toned vintage chairs and a characterful antique portrait. The dark grey of the painting links to the paint used on the lower section of the walls in the next-door bedroom and creates a seamless flow between the natural palettes.

CREATURE COMFORTS
Lynda's style combines natural finishes with simple, textural fabrics, cushions, sheepskin rugs and throws. Layered together, they bring a muted warmth that is both welcoming and cosy. The large contemporary armoire has been modified internally to hide the television while providing impact within the room.

HANDMADE STYLE
A traditional-looking oven, from Australian company Nectre, contrasts stylishly with the handmade concrete worktops, a poured concrete floor and contemporary artisanal lights. Open shelves provide valuable storage for Lynda's vast collections of old and new finds and kitchenalia.

The Estate appeals because?
It always feels as if you are in your own parkland.

Your style here is all about?
Relaxed comfort.

Most successful features?
Changing both the bathroom and kitchen to have a more contemporary feel within a very old house.

Best advice for designing a large country space?
Make sure you can throw off your shoes, curl up in a chair, lie on the couch, relax, rest and sleep. Comfort is key.

What quality time here means?
Quiet time. The views out of the window, the fresh vegetables and open garden are all a few steps away from the house – you can picnic well, cook with fresh ingredients, lie under a tree and get lost in the charm of it all.

Paint colour of choice?
A shade of white called Freesia by Wattyl.

What's on your walls?
One-third paint; wallpaper; old canvases and portraits, hung informally; a huge monochrome landscape; art propped on shelves; wall-to-wall kitchen shelves filled with old and new finds.

What's on your bedside table?
An old, tarnished silver jug (pitcher), filled with dried flowers.

Favourite possession here?
My art collections – random and accumulated over a lifetime.

Best seat in the house?
The huge couch and bathtub – both enjoy a garden view, through long windows.

What you couldn't live without?
The garden, the space around the house and the long driveway filled with trees – it touches me every time I return.

What tunes are playing?
Handsome Family, Leonard Cohen, Nick Cave, Tom Waits.

What's on the table for dinner?
Soup made from garden produce – the only time I love to cook!

Tell me something no one knows about this home?
The third bedroom was originally a potato-picker's tiny quarters. It is now one of the main features of the house and home to the largest bedroom. Totally separate, it looks onto the established vegetable gardens.

What noises can you hear?
Birds, dogs barking in the distance, the rustling of trees and leaves.

Scents evocative of here?
In the summer: fresh air, fragrant leaves and soil; in winter: the smoky fireplace and damp grass – all so special.

Favourite season at home?
All – they each evoke special times and memories.

This space makes you feel?
Instantly at home.

What are you dreaming up next?
To enjoy it more often.

VAULTED ELEGANCE
The white-painted, wood-clad walls in the converted potato shed add an elegant feel to the garden bedroom retreat. Peg rails provide a practical storage solution, helping to keep the room clutter-free and allowing the lofty space to retain a sense of calm.

OPEN TO IDEAS
The barn at The Estate is a delightful outbuilding that is available for location hire or to rent for weddings, parties, events and workshops. The vaulted structure was completely refurbished and insulated, and the classic form has taken on a new contemporary edge with concrete finishes and modern rustic furniture.

MAKING THE CUT
The seasonal garden produces year-round fruit and vegetable. It is surrounded by established olive trees, rosemary and sage, as well as a special tea garden for guests. The Estate is all about escaping city life and enjoying the relaxed ambience of a rural existence.

THE COTTAGE

Lynda Gardener

'The juxtaposition of old and new enhances the laid-back aesthetic – spaces are filled with pieces that I have been gathering since childhood and my early days with Levi Strauss.'

There is an almost hypnotic appeal to the interiors at The Cottage, an intimate three-bedroom bolthole that is testament to Lynda's ability to bring together colour, texture and all manner of collected curios. Rustic meets industrial, but curated with a distinctly contemporary edge.

White, as always, is the dominant colour of choice, yet throughout, the cottage is peppered with more dramatic touches: bedrooms decorated in coal-grey hues and chic monochrome toile; the library cocooned in a classic handmade wallpaper by Deborah Bowness; inky black wooden floors add depth to core living spaces; and blackboard-painted kitchen walls, displaying artfully written messages and recipes. The result is stylish and intriguing, yet immensely welcoming and thoughtful.

'The space was renovated 15 years ago and just keeps getting better with age,' says Lynda. 'I am a city girl through and through, but was ready to create an escape. Just 90 minutes from Melbourne, located within the picturesque spa town of Daylesford, The Cottage was my first country property and is used now

TABLE TALK

The salvaged green trestle dining table is framed by a collection of vintage boardroom chairs and oversized enamel pendant lights, all sourced by Lynda. The patina-rich, emerald-green armoire adds a sense of drama and unites the space with the garden beyond.

as one of my boutique rentals, next door to The Barn (see page 121). I still love to stay here – it reflects who I am and is never about decorating sensibly for guests.'

Despite the relaxed way in which Lynda has brought together each of the decorative elements in The Cottage, this is in no way an accidental success. Her enigmatic art of styling has been perfected: finds look as if they have always belonged – organic, quirky and never overly edited.

A former miner's cottage, built in the 1850s, the property had been poorly renovated 20 years ago. Yet despite it being run-down and overgrown, Lynda recognized fabulous bones beneath the ugly façade. At the front of the house, the rooms are original in size and scale, with reclaimed windows, doors and floorboards breathing new life back into the interior. At the centre of the house is the kitchen, a relaxed space with an antique draper's table-turned-island, concrete worktops and open shelves stacked high with beautiful white crockery. 'The kitchen leads into the open-plan sitting room and dining area, where three rooms were knocked into one to create a really large living space,' she says. 'Reclaimed finds abound: the boarded ceiling salvaged from a former factory; a set of five beautiful antique garden doors discovered at a local salvage yard; and fireplaces rebuilt with bricks rescued from the surrounding land.'

Lights play an important role throughout, affecting the mood as the day ebbs and flows. In the main bathroom a decadent French crystal chandelier hangs over an antique freestanding bathtub and adds a lingering sense of glamour to the rustic ambience. In the two main bedrooms and living areas industrial pendants and draped hanging bulbs add dynamic visual energy to personal schemes. Wooden shutters, made from old doors, filter a constant source of natural daylight. Practical, romantic and deliberate, they set the pared-back tone and act as a foil for the seasonally changing linens, textural furnishings and beautiful, timeworn furniture. 'The space is all about comfort,' smiles Lynda.

Outside, a former garage was converted into a pitched-roof garden bedroom, with vintage doors opening onto a leafy view. 'It has an inspiring sense of light and space: a private, one-room retreat, with its own claw-foot bathtub – the best spot to unwind in.'

Covetable collections hit you from every angle: it's the sort of home you crave time to wander around in on your own. Think tables stacked with interesting old books; glass domes encasing antique busts; vases filled with garden greenery; dressers (hutches) home to sculptures, trophies and select taxidermy; walls layered with art; and even a vintage typewriter, on which visitors can type heartfelt messages for the guestbook.

This is a home about spontaneous style – rediscovering the potential that others failed to see. It's the story of a derelict space brought back to life, with renewed vigour and a sincerity weaved through its timeless layers.

BENCHMARK STYLE
This raw, industrial kitchen has stood the test of time, combining both open shelving with bespoke concrete worktops and recycled taps (faucets). The moveable island provides a flexible yet stylish work surface, while the dramatic blackboard makes a quirky backdrop for guests' messages, recipes and inspirations.

1. Neck
2. Fore Ribs
3. Middle Ribs
4. Chuck Ribs
6. Rump
Cooked Prawn Risoni
bag of peas
Small can Sweet Corn (drained)
2 Sticks Celery Diced
Small onion (diced & Sauté in olive oil till caramelised)
Cooked Prawns
a handful chopped parsley
Mix all ingredients & season well with Salt & pepper

LILY BRETT
THE CITY
DOGBOY
FREDERICK FORSYTH
WILLIAM BOYD
DON WATSON
NICK HORNBY
THE EXCEPTION
LARSSON

DARK AND MOODY
Lynda converted a former bedroom into an intimate library with an altogether more masculine feel than the rest of the interior. The handmade wallpaper, by Deborah Bowness, adds a modern yet timeless vibe, offset by battered leather chairs and a vintage pendant light. Creative storytelling walls abound.

INNER CALM
The master bedroom is a relaxed and inviting oasis, dressed with luxurious linens and cosy textiles. Industrial lighting and a statement wallpaper panel, by Deborah Bowness, add a contemporary elegance to the pared-back room, while wooden shutters and simple garden sprigs lend an air of simplicity.

Gympie Third Grade National Football Club

The Cottage appeals because?
It was my first property in the country and the first brick miner's cottage to be built in the area – usually they are all weatherboard (clapboard).

Your style here is all about?
Moody spaces, dark floors and lots of favourite vintage pieces.

Most successful features?
The collections held within.

Best advice for designing a country cottage?
Keep it cosy, comfortable and warm: lots of big, fluffy feather cushions and the best natural linen sheets for the beds.

What quality time here means?
Total relaxation, with no plans.

Paint colour of choice?
Dulux Antique White U.S.A., and in the bedroom and library, moody colours by Porter's Paints.

What's on your walls?
Black-and-white toile and Deborah Bowness's 'Genuine Fake Bookshelf' wallpaper. Old oil paintings, collected locally, sketches, photographs, framed paintings and large art walls; leaning antique mirrors and blackboard kitchen walls.

What's on your bedside table?
I swap between the two bedrooms in the house; however, it almost always has a lamp and flowers picked from the garden.

Favourite possession here?
The antique French chandelier in the bathroom.

Best seat in the house?
My leather chairs in the library. Surrounded by books, this is the perfect place for a nightcap.

What you couldn't live without?
The textures and original details. I kept all I could, including cracks and uneven walls – everything that makes this place so special.

What tunes are playing?
Thom Yorke, alt-J, Placebo.

What's on the table for dinner?
I always invite a friend to stay, who loves to cook – so supper is usually a surprise!

Tell me something no one knows about this home?
The house had been left up for sale for more than a year – to the naked eye, it had no real redeeming features, but to me it had huge potential.

What noises can you hear?
Birds, trees and occasional passing cars.

Scents evocative of here?
The fireplace – the aroma of burning wood seems to have permeated the walls and furniture over the years and instantly reminds me I am in the country.

Favourite season at home?
Winter, with the fires lit.

This space makes you feel?
Instantly relaxed.

What are you dreaming up next?
Just enjoying it as it is. The look is timeless, and it seems to have found its permanent rhythm and style.

LOFTY HEIGHTS
The garden room, home to a one-room bed-and-bath escape, has a spacious light-filled ambience, with an effortless mix of old and new. The industrial fan, old medicine cabinet and claw-foot bathtub reflect Lynda's signature style and are juxtaposed with newer textile finds and contemporary overhead lighting.

METAL WORKS
The claw-foot iron bathtub is Lynda's perfect place to unwind. The large antique mirror bounces light around the whitewashed space, while an ornate French chandelier adds a feminine contrast to the industrial bulb pendant light, 1930s scales and vintage medicine cabinet.

ALBION

THE SHED

Fran Derham + Michael Robertson

'By harnessing the power of creative collaborations, we have achieved a minimalistic, yet highly sophisticated design that intuitively links to the landscape.'

This striking rural home, owned by Fran Derham and Michael Robertson, is a lesson in nurturing the seed of an idea until it surpasses the original vision and becomes something altogether different, yet better. The Wensley, known affectionately as The Shed, is located high on the rolling hills of rural Victoria, in Wensleydale, on the Surf Coast Hinterland of Australia, a 20-minute drive to the iconic Great Ocean Road. The property, set within a dramatic 32-hectare (80-acre) farm, blends perfectly with the natural vernacular.

Within the design and build, the couple has channelled their dream of creating a unique family bolthole, which doubles at times as an exclusive Airbnb retreat that sleeps ten. Their approach to curating their home is somewhat different from Lynda's more eclectic style; here, the look is sparse and collections are limited. But what gives this home its character and a sense of unity is the use of one material: wood. Wood is ever-present within the home, it provides the raw ingredient used for both the build and bespoke storage; the textural palette that informs all the spaces; the frame for the breathtaking

WOOD EDIT

The utilitarian, natural interior feels alive with breathable materials that will look even better with age. In the dining area, earthy textural surfaces, including weathered wood and concrete, give impact to the pared-back ambience. This sense of timeless beauty adds a sustainable appeal.

picture windows that negate the need for art; a repurposing of Michael's long-collected salvaged timber stock; and a seamless link to nature. 'Timber lies at the heart of it all: we have worked hard to keep clutter at bay, allowing the materials and architecture to inform the space,' explains Fran.

The mix of Oregon (Douglas Fir), ironbark, silvertop ash and Australian hardwood timber, the surrounding earthy ambience and underfoot organic warmth exudes a restful calm. Interestingly, throughout the entire space, not one plastered or painted wall breaks the flow. 'There is a softness and subtleness to the timber: it moves and changes colour seasonally, and as you enter, the building immediately cocoons you. At night, with pitch-black skies, the wood lends an overwhelming quiet to spaces and sleep,' she says.

Fran, a producer, had grown up spending summers nearby and, together, the couple had fostered a love of this area. 'In 2010, Michael went out for a drive and came back saying that he had found the perfect spot to build a getaway. We both instantly connected with the seclusion and land.' The idea for the build began as a passion project for Michael – a builder, with a desire to create his own contemporary take on the iconic Australian shed. At weekends, for four years, the couple lived in their caravan on the land. 'We wanted to get to know the landscape, the views and to work out how the seasons affected the plot, so we were happy to take our time. The house resonates with personal meaning: it is where Michael proposed to me and feels very pivotal to our connection with each other, and now to our children too,' says Fran.

No strangers to renovating, this was, however, the couple's first new build. Michael, inspired by time spent in Montana, USA, and the couple's shared passion for skiing, was drawn to the log cabin style of luxury mountain retreats, as well as the iconic Kempsey House, New South Wales, built by architect Glenn Murcutt in 1974. To help bring ideas to life, they commissioned their friend, architect Nick Byrne. 'Nick, well-known for his clean-lined contemporary designs and sculptural angles, collaborated with us and the interior designer Lisa Buxton, who helped us add an international edge to the rustic interiors.'

The design marries two connecting buildings: one shed the home and the other a store, with potential for future projects. The natural cross ventilation from the striking glazing – integral to the success of this build – unites nature and structure. The monolithic concrete sculpture, adjacent to the wood-burning stove, creates a sense of drama and can be enjoyed from every angle, both in the downstairs open-plan layout and in the upstairs galleried loft – home to a fun bunk room that sleeps six. 'Sitting by the fire, taking in the view and the beauty of what we have created together, feels very humbling,' Fran reflects.

Throughout the open-plan design, a sophisticated kitchen and glamorous bathrooms are complemented by contemporary lighting, organic textiles and sustainable textures. 'The build will get even better with age and will, we hope, be nurtured for generations to come,' says Fran.

ALL IN THE DETAIL
Every nuance within the build has been carefully considered. The kitchen features a Falcon range cooker, hand-painted wooden units with bespoke leather handles, and open shelves displaying earthy crockery and practical utensils that create visual interest within the minimal interior.

WOOD HOUSES

The Shed appeals because?
It has been built entirely out of natural materials.

Your style here is all about?
I'm a bit of a chameleon, so my style depends on the bones of the house. We built this space and my husband was the driving force behind the rustic aesthetic and the use of all the timber. My touch is adding the understated luxury – everything you need in the right place.

Most successful features?
The views. The kitchen and the lounge are incredible to be in because of the large floor-to-ceiling windows.

What's your best advice for designing a shed?
Get to know the land, where the light falls during each season and what the views are like from different spots on the property, no matter how big or small.

What quality time here means?
Family and outdoors.

Paint colour of choice?
The only paint we have is on the kitchen joinery – Squid Ink, by Porter's Paints. Everything else is recycled Oregon and new ironbark.

What's on your walls?
It's all about the wood and the picture window vista.

What's on your bedside table?
Lamps with bespoke shades, created from antique French fabric bolts, by Lisa Buxton Interiors.

Favourite possession here?
The Cheminées Philippe fireplace.

Biggest extravagance?
The store shed; it's twice the size of the house – a proper man cave.

Best seat in the house?
The couch by the fire – on a full moon or at sunrise. Take your pick!

What you couldn't live without?
The views.

What tunes are playing?
Always a playlist. A few of my favourite songs: 'Palaces of Montezuma', Grinderman; 'Wolf Like Me', TV On The Radio; 'Slide Away', Miley Cyrus; 'To Leave Something Behind', Sean Rowe; and 'The Heart Is a Muscle', Gang of Youths.

What's on the table for dinner?
Often it's Nigella Lawson's Mirin-Glazed Salmon.

Tell me something no one knows about this home?
It was meant to be a tiny shack made of recyclable material, but my husband and our architect got carried away. Eyeroll.

What noises can you hear?
Frogs and the wind.

Scents evocative of here?
It's pretty musky, to be honest. The Oregon is uncoated and secretes a woody scent. But when you open the windows, wet grass and gum from the trees.

Favourite season at home?
Autumn.

This space makes you feel?
At peace.

What are you dreaming up next?
A natural swimming hole/billabong in one of our dams. Imagine huge slabs of rock jutting out into a deep green pool, with a sandy beach and perhaps a rope swing from a friendly gum tree.

RUSTIC ELEGANCE
The low-ceilinged, wood-clad attic bedroom contrasts with the lofty main living areas and creates a cocooning place of rest. Outside, a French antique iron bathtub and shower have been installed on a secluded deck. The sense of oneness with the surrounding landscape creates a beguiling escape.

STUDIO
SALLY COULTHARD
THE KINFOLK HOME
A FRAME FOR LIFE
ILSE
SIROTA
GUESS WHO
STEIDL

THE TOWNHOUSE

Ali + Ian Heath

'Our home has a sense of longevity and connection that appeals. With the passing of time, this has become even more significant and meaningful.'

For me, home is the foundation of everything, the place where I can be true to myself, surrounded by family, and where I feel relaxed and creative. It has been at the start of many new journeys: moving in when it was just my husband and me; leaving the corporate world to open an antique and interior company; providing the catalyst for my move into styling and journalism; falling pregnant with our two children; and celebrating endless happy occasions. We have been here for nearly two decades – but things have never stood still.

Located in the heart of an historic market town in Surrey, England, our Georgian home was built in 1750. The 18th-century painted façade, surrounded by original decorative railings, gives way at the back to a brick exterior and charming walled garden. Within an urban setting, this hidden courtyard – full of established olive trees, a giant magnolia and lots of seasonal planting – feels both a surprise and a luxury.

We fell in love with the house for its symmetrical proportions, the light-filled orangery at the end of the kitchen, and the period details: an original

TAKE A SEAT

Natural textures abound, with antique linen and velvet upholstery, and handmade cushions in vintage monogrammed linen and antique striped hemp. The French decorative mirror juxtaposes with a Danish mid-century coffee table by Poul Kjærholm and abundant ceramics.

central staircase, fireplaces and shuttered sash windows. With four bedrooms over three storeys, there are lots of nooks and unexpected turns. The house seems to expand as you work your way up to the top floor, which is home to a lofty sitting room, an office and a fourth bedroom.

Our home has become more pared back over time and in 2017 we renovated and reconfigured spaces, adding a new kitchen and new bathrooms. I always try to combine function and form with a sense of authenticity – that is important to me. Spaces work hard, displays constantly evolve and furniture regularly changes rooms. This is a place in which we love to entertain and gather, so everything is used and enjoyed.

The spaces feature a blend of natural materials: wide oak boards, marble, and limestone. Their soulful patinas fit with the house and will look even better as time passes. I see so much colour at work that the knocked-back palette at home is both restful and calming – a chalky mix of whites, soft greys and deeper earthier tones, balanced with shades of tobacco, brown and black. I love the way simple monochrome schemes allow furniture, collections and art to stand out, and work comfortably alongside both old and new finds.

Natural, textured fabrics, with character and imperfections, always appeal; there is a beauty in their timeworn appearance and a sense of provenance that resonates. Throughout the house, old sofas, chairs and light shades have been re-covered in antique linen, and many vintage pieces have been sourced on travels to different countries.

I have an appreciation of things made by hand: cushions, quilts and bolsters made from repurposed hemp sacks, antique fabrics and intricately handstitched monogrammed sheets; hand-carved wooden spoons; and handcrafted ceramics. Astier de Villatte is a favourite homeware brand of mine – each piece a work of art, made by hand in Paris.

For me, natural finds add a restorative energy, so throughout the house collections of antique coral, sea ferns and seashells, brought home from family trips, are displayed alongside sculptural, dried foliage. Books are stacked everywhere – on consoles, shelves and floors; there are too many, but they are a vital part of what makes me tick.

My style has definitely simplified over the years – I like to mix a few investment pieces with carefully sourced inexpensive finds. Everything here recalls a memory, from the abstract painting Ian bought for me from a street seller in New York to the French bed and mirrors sourced during my early days buying antiques, and the many pieces bought from creatives I have enjoyed writing about. I am a passionate collector, always in search of new makers, independent sellers, antique haunts, markets and galleries – the buzz of discovering something special never fades. For me, it is those unique finds that make rooms feel individual – they are part of our story and what makes this home.

I never forget that the word 'home' can be charged with emotion for many: I feel very lucky to share this one with my family and never take that for granted.

CABINET OF CURIOSITIES
Treasured finds are displayed in stylish vignettes around the home. Edited selections of ceramics, natural finds, mercurized glassware, Fornasetti candles and all manner of whimsical curios are displayed in the sitting room bookcase. The monochrome palette unifies the collected treasures.

SALLY COULTHARD
KINFOLK HOME
S WHO
STEIDL

IN THE FRAME
A collection of antique botanical prints, mounted onto linen backing within bespoke frames, creates a striking picture wall in the dining room. A carved wooden table and handmade linen-covered chairs offset a footed bowl by Astier de Villatte and select antique finds.

The Townhouse appeals because?
The house has a soul that is hard to explain – it feels like part of who I am.

Your style here is all about?
Pared-back tones, earthy textures, collections and comfort. Lived-in, timeworn and hugely personal.

Most successful features?
The laundry on the middle floor – it's life-changing!

Best advice for designing a townhouse?
Keep things simple, stick to a select palette of colours and only choose things you truly love.

What quality time here means?
A place for creativity, the important people in my life and the start of many dreams – such as writing this book.

Paint colour of choice?
Farrow & Ball – all of the shades between All White and Mole's Breath.

What's on your walls?
A complete mix of contemporary abstracts, old prints, antique portraits, maps and vintage finds. I have promised to leave Lynda my antique male portraits one day.

What's on your bedside table?
Diptyque and Mad et Len candles, and always books.

Favourite possession here?
So many! Letters from my late dad; pebbles from Nantucket, Massachusetts; Astier de Villatte everything; and my children's plaster teeth moulds – a reminder of how their faces have changed!

Best seat in the house?
The kitchen island – it's where every important conversation takes place.

What you couldn't live without?
My husband, children and our dog, Purdey – they make our home complete.

What tunes are playing?
Max Richter and Michael Nyman when I'm writing; Gregory Porter and Nina Simone when I'm relaxing; and so much I have no control over!

What's on the table for dinner?
Always a surprise – my gorgeous husband is a great cook. My suppers never quite hit the mark.

Tell me something no one knows about this home?
It started life as a brewer's house and has been home to a few notorious characters.

What noises can you hear?
Passers-by, music from the park and birds. We have a huge magnolia tree and vertically planted courtyard walls full of nests.

Scents evocative of here?
Ernesto by Cire Trudon, Sang Bleu by Mad et Len; and for me, Thé Noir 29 by Le Labo – it's a definite love affair.

Favourite season at home?
In summer the garden comes alive and is where we spend all our time. In winter the house is the perfect place to hunker down with the fire lit.

This space makes you feel?
Myself, happy and always appreciative.

What are you dreaming up next?
Creating an office outdoors that links back into the house.

ART + SOUL
Collections of pots, both old and new, take centre stage throughout the house. A reclaimed console table is home to stacks of books and the contemporary handmade *Elliptoid Vessel*, a treasured Hannah Tounsend creation. Textural finishes, artworks and carved wooden details add layers of interest within the earthy spaces.

WABI-SABI WELCOME
Wreaths
CREATIVE HOME
The Foraged Home
NEW LONDON STYLE
LIVE BEAUTIFUL
WHITE
Quiet Pattern
CHRISTIAN DIOR
IMPRINTS
a life less ordinary
EAT DRINK NAP
Surf Shacks
the stuff of life
monochrome home
La Lumière et les Oiseaux
It's beautiful here
Megan Morton
ANTONY GORMLEY
HAUTE BOHEMIANS
TRAVEL HOME
etcetera
Sibella Court
NOMAD
Inspired by Nature
THE NATURAL HOME
A TREE IN THE HOUSE · HICKSON
the maker
The Magpie & the Wardrobe
Creative Living London
THE VINTAGE MODERN HOME
MODIGLIANI
THE ORIGINALS
THE ALCHEMY OF THINGS
THE MAVERICK SOUL
SHE
Axel Vervoordt
Portraits of Interiors
Up & Down New York
ESSENTIAL HOUSE BOOK

14

TEXTURAL EDGE
The master en-suite is a blend of old-meets-new – concrete surfaces, unpolished brassware and contemporary lighting are offset with antique portraits and vintage stoneware. In the master bedroom an antique French headboard is juxtaposed with hand-dyed velvet cushions by Kirsten Hecktermann, natural linens and a Caroline Popham abstract painting.

THE RETREAT

Marnie + Ryan Hawson

'Every time I make a decision about my home, it is based on my values of living a sustainable life. The choices become simple and intuitive.'

Within the home of photographer Marnie Hawson, a series of intimate, calming spaces unfold, which embody her desire to nurture a more sustainable existence, both in the way she lives and chooses to work. Having enjoyed a previous career as an environmental scientist, Marnie switched to a more creative role, working as an interior, travel and lifestyle photographer, specializing in work for clients who are both environmentally and ethically aware. This was a dramatic shift, but one firmly wrapped up in the idea that mindful decisions equate to a better quality of life and, in turn, personal contentment.

The four-bedroom home, which Marnie shares with her husband Ryan and their miniature pinscher Dexter, has a tranquil and authentic feel. It is a place where decorative choices are made based on comfort, visual aesthetics and personal codes of practice. Paints are zero VOC, the energy supply is 100 per cent carbon neutral, organic vegetables and fruits grow plentifully outside, Belgian d'Uccle chickens roam free, and products are chosen for their longevity and sustainability merits.

ART OF SIMPLICITY

A welcoming wood-burning stove creates a focal point within the open-plan kitchen and dining area, which leads out to the garden beyond. The vintage table is surrounded by a set of 1930s Thonet 'Czech' chairs, and the white walls, cabinets and voiles create an airy, light elegance.

'My ethos is always to buy pieces that will stand the test of time. It is never about trends or value; always an object's history, the story behind how it was made, or its connection to my life.' One such example is the collection of vintage horse sketches and oils, which remind Marnie of her teenage years, when she competed as a national three-day eventer.

In 2010 the couple returned from a year spent driving across Europe in their motor home. 'It was an amazing adventure, but by the end we were very keen to put down some roots and buy a house,' says Marnie. 'Our criteria for a home was simple. We wanted an old country property, full of character, quirks and a sense of history.'

This charming weatherboard (clapboard) cottage, built in the 1890s, hit the mark immediately. Nestled in the picturesque hamlet of Riddells Creek, an hour's drive from Melbourne, it is situated on the main street, where large gaggles of wild geese frequently wander by. From the traditional front veranda, views are enjoyed across to an open paddock and lake, and from the back, up to the Macedon Ranges. Drawn to the colours of the surrounding scrubby bushland – full of kangaroos, birds and wildlife – the couple have layered their whitewashed home in a palette of wheat, warm ochre and gentle greens, combined with soft greys and earthy browns. Indigenous foraged finds and natural textures fill their home: think organic linens, aged wood furniture, natural jute rugs and an abundance of nature-inspired artworks.

Spaces needed some love decoratively, but many of the original features had survived, including the wooden panelling and claw-foot bathtub. Changes have been completed gradually, as time allowed and tastes evolved. In the kitchen, a 50-year-old Aga, discovered on Gumtree, now forms the heart of the home and was the catalyst for the kitchen update. An upcycled Czech tub and antique brass taps (faucets) transformed the sink area, while simple Ikea cabinetry was given a contemporary lift with bespoke concrete worktops and new open shelves for decorative displays.

'To me, spaces should develop over time. There is something special about waiting to find the right elements, not rushing to finish everything in a few weeks,' explains Marnie. 'We have chosen to buy everything second-hand, upcycled or from companies that value the importance of ethical craftsmanship and timeless natural materials. Things are here to stay, so we wanted to make the right choices first time.'

The most recent updates included the renovation of the former village post office, which came as part of the property. 'After we moved in, we discovered the original post office boxes up for sale; they now have pride of place in the house. Their timeworn metal patina is very special,' says Marnie. The space has been converted into an atmospheric bar-meets-den: 'It's the best space for entertaining, and the moody hues contrast with the lighter feel of the house.'

'Home is where we relax and feel our most fulfilled. A great sense of satisfaction comes with knowing that we are restoring our cottage as a true reflection of who we are and how we choose to live.'

MAIN EVENT
The reclaimed white-enamelled Aga is Marnie's favourite piece and takes pride of place in the family's kitchen. Concrete worktops, a utilitarian pendant light and an interesting collection of eclectic decorative finds add an individual appeal to the whitewashed kitchen space.

AGA

USE
MBARNAILS

SHELF LIFE
Half-panelled kitchen walls create an opportunity for creative displays of practical utensils, vintage kitchenalia and favourite collectables, including a small painting that was a gift from Marnie's mother. Ever-changing foraged finds are displayed throughout, adding textural and tactile appeal.

SHIRE OF GISBORNE
POUND ACT 1958
GISBORNE POUND
POUND FEES
DESCRIPTION OF CATTLE
AMOUNT
$ C
FOR EVERY SHEEP 0·20
FOR EVERY HEAD OF OTHER CATTLE 3·00
ADDITIONAL CHARGES
AMOUNT
$ C
FOR WRITING AND DELIVERING OR SENDING BY POST ANY NOTICE 2.00
FOR INSERTING ANY NOTICE IN THE GOVERNMENT GAZETTE AND A NEWSPAPER IN ADDITION TO THE ACTUAL COST OF SUCH INSERTION 2.00
FOR INSPECTION OF POUND BOOK 5.00
FOR REGISTRATION OF BRANDS & MARKS 5.00
I. H. LARKINS
POUNDKEEPER
TABLE OF RATES TO BE CHARGED FOR
TO THE POUND WHERE MOTOR TRANSPORT IS
IMPOUNDED. FIXED BY THE COUNCIL OF THE
A FOR TRESPASS
DESCRIPTION OF CATTLE TRESPASSING
FOR EVERY SHEEP
FOR EVERY GOAT
FOR EVERY PIG
FOR EVERY HEAD OF OTHER CATTLE
B FOR TRANSPORT
DESCRIPTION OF CATTLE
FOR EVERY SHEEP
FOR EVERY HEAD OF OTHER CATTLE
C FOR SUSTENANCE
DESCRIPTION OF CATTLE
FOR EVERY SHEEP
FOR EVERY GOAT
FOR EVERY PIG
FOR EVERY HEAD OF OTHER CATTLE

The Retreat appeals because?
It's a country cottage, but it's connected to the community. You can enjoy an evening drink in the front yard, listening to the geese honking, while chatting to all the locals walking by.

Your style here is all about?
Sustainability, good design and functionality – always with neutral colours and natural materials.

Most successful features?
The wooden clothes airer, which hangs above the wood fire in the living room. Genius design!

What's your best advice for designing a retreat?
Create zones, both within and outside the house, for different activities and energy levels.

What quality time here means?
Relaxing and retreating from the outside world – this is a true haven where we can be ourselves and enjoy each other's company. And hosting others when we are feeling sociable.

Paint colour of choice?
Mostly Dulux Antique White U.S.A., but with more touches of darkness creeping in, Bauwerk Colour's Tumble is a favourite.

What's on your walls?
Art collected from different parts of the world, old clocks and as much brassware as I can fit.

What's on your bedside table?
Always fresh flowers, hand cream, lip balm and an empty coffee cup in the mornings.

Favourite possession here?
The Aga stove has a special place in our hearts, as we had an 'Aga fund' for our wedding, after falling in love with these beauties while travelling overseas. This old girl will stay with the house if we move; the next one needs to run off renewable energy.

Biggest extravagance?
A private bar full of single malt whisky in the front garden, dubbed the Misses Sutherlands, to honour the two spinster sisters who lived in our home and ran the post office for 50 years.

Best seat in the house?
The custom, upholstered window seat, built by our good friend. It's next to the Aga and looks out onto the veggie garden.

What you couldn't live without?
My darling husband – home is wherever he is.

What tunes are playing?
Always The National, always.

What's on the table for dinner?
Anything veggie, with ingredients from the garden when we can.

Tell me something no one knows about this home?
Rumour has it, one of the front bedrooms was once used as a bank. More recently, one of the owners had more than 100 cats.

What noises can you hear?
Kookaburras in the garden and the country train hurtling past every now and again.

Scents evocative of here?
Wood smoke, whisky and the fresh air of the Australian landscape.

Favourite season at home?
Spring – the wood fire and Aga are still going, but the chill is out of the air and the doors can be flung open on a good day.

This space makes you feel?
Calm. Happy. Content.

What are you dreaming up next?
Wild, bee-friendly flowerbeds at the back of the house; dark, moody bedrooms with brass hardware and French ceramic pendants.

BED + BATH
Recycled vintage shoe lasts add a quirky backdrop within the master bedroom and offset the original whitewashed panelled walls. Layers of gorgeously crumpled linens give a relaxed feel, while fresh, natural greenery lends a sense of vitality to the pared-back spaces.

YOUR JOURNEY

If we wanted you to take one thing away from this book, we hope it is recognizing the importance of storytelling and living your life in the way that best reflects you. This modern rustic way of curating a home is just one of a huge number of styles and possibilities, but what is key to everything is that the process described in *Curate* can be applied to any space, budget or style.

Creating a home through interior design and interior styling does not need to be a daunting prospect if you listen to your heart, follow some guidance and, if desired, choose a specialist with whom to collaborate. After all, we all have skills that make us shine in different ways, and if asking for help means someone enables you to see your treasures in a new light, then that is a gift too.

When your home reflects how you live, how you want your spaces to be, and you are surrounded by things you want to enjoy every day, it changes everything. You will be listening to the real you, the authentic you – when life is short and so precious, that is really important. Your senses will be triggered by everything you see, smell, touch and even hear. Remember, each of those triggers is hugely personal, because this is your story.

We are very grateful that you have taken the time to buy our book and explore its pages. Across two sides of the world, our collaboration has been everything, and we hope it highlights the importance of a life well lived.

So, own your look, allow yourself the space to be creative, be true to your style and, above all, enjoy wherever it is that you call home: whether that be your first apartment, your ultimate-goal space or a tiny hut in the middle of nowhere. The point is to have a dream, to own your story and to let your journey evolve.

Ali + Lynda x x

'Nurture carefully
the home you are curating.
It should feel like the nest of your dreams.'

SHOP

SOURCES UK

Alex Eagle Studio
alexeagle.co.uk

Alex MacArthur Interiors
alexmacarthur.co.uk

Anton & K Antiques
antonandk.co.uk

AU Bespoke
aubespoke.com

Baileys Home & Garden
baileyshome.com

Brownrigg
brownrigg-interiors.co.uk

Chloe Antiques
chloeantiques.com

Decorative Antiques UK
decorativeantiquesuk.com

Design Vintage
designvintage.co.uk

Domestic Science
domesticsciencehome.co.uk

Emma Leschallas Antiques
leschallas-antiques.co.uk

The Fig Store
thefigstore.com

Gilli Hanna Decorative Antiques
gillihanna-antiques.co.uk

Giovanna Ticciati
giovannaticciati.com

Haus
haus-interiors.co.uk

Hill & Co Home
hillandcohome.co.uk

Josephine Ryan Antiques
josephineryanantiques.co.uk

Liberty
libertylondon.com

Maison Artefact
maisonartefact.com

Nām
namstore.co.uk

Petersham Nurseries
petershamnurseries.com

Puckhaber Decorative Antiques
puckhaberdecorativeantiques.com

Retrouvius
retrouvius.com

Skinflint Lighting
skinflintdesign.com

Streett Marburg
streettmarburg.co.uk

The Country Brocante
thecountrybrocante.co.uk

The Hambledon
thehambledon.com

The King & I
tkandishop.com

Vanil
vanil.co.uk

Wattle & Daub
wattleanddaubhome.co.uk

SOURCES US

abc carpet & home
abchome.com

Armadillo
usa.armadillo-co.com

Bloomist
bloomist.com

Dear: Rivington +
dearrivington.com

Homes Stories
homestories.com

Roman and Williams Guild
rwguild.com

SOURCES AUSTRALIA

Bed Threads
bedthreads.com.au

Caro Melbourne
caromelbourne.com

Cibi
cibi.com.au

Loom Towels
loomtowels.com

Manon Bis
manonbis.com.au

Major-Minor
majorminorwares.com

The Plant Society
theplantsociety.com.au

Scout House
scouthouse.com.au

The Dharma Door
thedharmadoor.com.au

The Hub General Store
thehubgeneralstore.com.au

The Panton Store
shop.shelleypanton.com

Tigmi Trading
tigmitrading.com

SOURCES EUROPE

101 Copenhagen
101cph.com

Astier de Villatte
astierdevillatte.com

Casa González & González
gonzalez-gonzalez.es

Graanmarkt 13
graanmarkt13.com

Merci Paris
merci-merci.com

Studio Oliver Gustav
olivergustav.com

WORLDWIDE

Aesop
aesop.com

Le Labo Fragrances
lelabofragrances.com

FOLLOW

@1924us
Antiques + Writing + Film + Design + Makers

@astylistguide
Kitchen + Interior Stylist

@bauwerkcolour
Natural Limewash Paint Company

@blackshorestyle
Interior Stylist + Set Design + Creative Direction

@caro_melbourne
Retailer

@carolinepopham
Artist

@casaatica
Furniture + Architectural Design

@cathypentonatelier
Designer + Maker

@colinking
Stylist + Designer

@deborah_bowness
Designer + Hand-Printed Wallpapers

@elvis_robertson_ceramics
Plate Maker

@eyeswoon
Interior Designer + Author

@fabulousvintagefinds
Vintage Wares

@francisgallery
Art Gallery

@glenproebstel
Creative Director + Set Designer + Interior Stylist

@hana.snow
Interior Stylist + Art Director

@hannah_tounsend
Ceramicist + Printmaker

@hansblomquist
Stylist + Art Direction + Author

@hilaryrobertson
Author + Interior Stylist + Set Designer

@houseofgreylondon
Interior Design + Creative Direction + Styling

@igigigeneralstore
Antiques + Homeware + Fashion

@ingredientsldn
Online Homeware

@kararosenlund
Stylist + Photographer + Author

@leantimms
Travel + Lifestyle Photographer + Storyteller

@mad_about_the_house
Author + Journalist + Blogger

@maison_hand_fr
Studio + Interior Design + Editions + Lifestyle

@malenebirgers_world
Design + Fashion + Interiors + Art

@marialemesurier
Designer + Stylist

@martynthompsonstudio
Designer + Photographer + Creative Director

@megan_morton
Interior Stylist + Author

@monogiraud
Artist

@mrjasongrant
Stylist + Designer + Author

@nataliewalton
Stylist + Shopkeeper + Author

@nielsmaier_
Interior Design

@nookvintage
Antique Dealer

@oysterbridgeandco
Artist

@plumesandfeathers
Trend Boards

@robwynyates.studio
Abstract Painter

@ruthribeaucourt
Founder of The French Muse + Editor

@saarmanche
Artist

@sarahandrews.co
Stylist + Interior Designer

@sibellacourt
Interior + Product Designer + Author

@studioanoukb
Interior Design + Style Studio

@thedesignfiles
Design Blog Site

@thehiddenhut
Interiors + Lifestyle Hut

@thefuturekept
Consciously Crafted + Sustainable + Ethical Goods

@theoscarcollective
Decorative Antiques

@tinystories.nl
Artist

@viamartine
Poster + Print Studio

@verdenius
Lifestyle + Interior + Food Photographer

@waynepate
Artist

INDEX

Page numbers in *italics* refer to illustrations

INDEX

THE TEAM

About the Interior Stylist
Lynda Gardener is an Australia-based interior stylist. She has been credited internationally as the founder of one of the first global lifestyle stores, Empire, which she started in her twenties in Melbourne and ran successfully for more than two decades. Simultaneously, for the past 30 years, she has slowly built a portfolio of boutique accommodation, which has become synonymous with her eclectic style, collector's eye and desire for the unique. Lynda also consults on design and interior styling for both commercial and residential projects, in Australia and abroad. Her work is regularly featured in high-profile international publications including *Country Style, Elle Decoration, Homes & Gardens, Livingetc, Modern Rustic, Vogue Living* and *VT Wonen*.
Instagram @lynda.gardener
www.lyndagardener.com

About the Writer
Ali Heath is a UK-based interiors writer, stylist and content creator, who has more than 16 years' freelance experience working with prestigious interior and lifestyle magazines. Her work is featured regularly in many notable titles including *Country Living, Elle Decoration, Elle Decoration Country, Homes & Gardens, House & Garden, Livingetc, Modern Rustic, Red*, the *Telegraph* and *YOU Magazine*. She collaborates with various leading photographers, and her work is also syndicated internationally. Prior to going freelance, Ali set up a successful antiques business, after working as new business director for a top marketing agency.
Instagram @aliheath_uk
www.aliheath.co.uk

About the Photographer
Marnie Hawson is an Australia-based international interiors, travel and lifestyle photographer. Her work is published in many of the world's top interiors magazines, including *Australian House & Garden, Condé Nast Traveller, Country Style, Elle Decoration, Gourmet Traveller, Green, Habitus, Harper's Bazaar, Home Beautiful, Homes & Garden, Livingetc* and *Real Living*. A former environmental scientist, she now focuses her work on purpose-driven photography for people doing good things. As a team, Marnie, Lynda and Ali regularly collaborate for publications in the UK, and Marnie is represented internationally by Living Inside agency, in Milan.
Instagram @marniehawson
www.marniehawson.com.au

THANK YOU

Creating this book has been the realization of a long-held ambition for us both. Yet neither the book nor our careers would ever have been possible without the support of all of the amazing mentors, editors, photographers, stylists, designers, creatives, homeowners, shopkeepers, clients and followers, whose mutual worlds and friendship we have shared over the years. It is because of you that both our journeys were made possible. We are eternally grateful for that love, support and encouragement, and never take it for granted.

Firstly, to our publisher, Alison Starling at Octopus, thank you for having faith in the original concept pitched and for your support in making this process so enjoyable. Allowing me and Lynda the ability to inject our creative energy, ideas and style into these pages has been so appreciated. You gave me advice as a publisher all those years ago, so for our paths to have crossed again and for this book, a first for us both, to be with you, feels very serendipitous. Thank you also to Jonathan Christie for bringing our ideas, images, flat plan and words to life, and creating a book of which we are very proud. And to our great editor Faye Robson, tireless production manager Katherine Hockley and the broader Octopus team, for getting our book out there, we are so very grateful.

A huge thank you to our brilliant photographer, Marnie Hawson, for the truly beautiful images. Alun Callender, thank you for your stunning work; your support has meant a lot. We are grateful to Fran Derham and Michael Robertson for sharing their home; and Carley Spooner and Tamara Maynes for allowing us to feature shots within Est Studios. Thank you also to the lovely Nikki Griffiths, Belle Hemming and Erin Malloy for all your valuable contributions. To all the creatives, readers and shopkeepers who have bought and endorsed this book, including Martyn Thompson and Kate Watson-Smyth – thank you, it means the world.

ALI

To Lynda, thank you from the bottom of my heart. Our collaboration started as a glimmer of an idea and I have loved working with you, but above all treasure the friendship that has come out of it. I will never forget the late night/early morning calls from the UK to Australia, and all the stories and laughter. Your intuitive styling, sense of fun, kindness and down-to-earth take on life are infectious, and the steadfast commitment to each other has been very special.

A huge thank you to my beautiful husband, Ian. You are my everything – a constant sounding board in my life – and your love, belief, support and amazing cooking throughout the process of writing this book have been hugely appreciated – you are the best! My gorgeous children, Grace and Archie, you are my world – thank you for making me laugh during this busy project. Your love and sense of fun are what makes our house a home. Thank you to my parents for bringing us up in such a happy childhood home; my gorgeous sister, Ju, for your endless encouragement and always being there for me; and my mother-in-law, Rose, for always caring.

I feel very blessed to have all my gorgeous friends – I am beyond lucky to have you in my life and treasure our friendships and your support deeply. Being surrounded by so much talent in our industry is a gift, and one that continually inspires. It is a privilege to have made so many close creative work contacts, many of whom I now call friends – thank you for everything over the years.

I would like to dedicate this book to my very special Dad and father-in-law, who are sadly no longer with us. You both created such nurturing homes and gave me the confidence to believe in myself, dream big, aim high and to always be kind along the way. I can never thank you enough.

LYNDA

Previously I could have only dreamed about being a part of something so special; yet here we are, writing the acknowledgements for these pages. Without the support, care and goodness from all involved, starting with Ali, this would have never been. I am forever grateful for your love, vision and devotion in wanting to create this book together – a friend for life! It was humbling to be asked to be a part of this collaboration and I will cherish the experience forever. It's an honour to work with such talent and I feel utterly privileged.

Thank you to my friends, who mean the world to me and are always there to support me, through thick and thin. As we know, friendship, or 'our family' (as we prefer to call it), is everything.

To my two sisters, Marina and Arlene, thank you for always listening and being there, day and night.

To my partners throughout my life, who always allowed me to follow my desires, dreams and goals – you have been such an important part of my story, and I love and appreciate you so much.

To my peers, who I admire more than anything – we all grew up together, watching each other's careers develop. Your support and love, for so many years, has carried me through and cannot ever be truly described: Mikkel Vang, Louella Boitel-Gill, Lisa Cohen, Karen McCartney, Sibella Court, Glen Proebstel, Sharyn Cairns, Megan Morton, Kara Rosenlund, Annemarie Kiely, Jason Grant, Tamara Maynes, Lucy Feagins and so many more.

My mother set the benchmark so high with her interior flair, making our homes such special places in which to live. Thank you to my parents for encouraging me to be who I am today; and for never doubting me and my many crazy goals. I dedicate this book to you both.

An Hachette UK Company
www.hachette.co.uk

First published in Great Britain in 2021 by Mitchell Beazley, an imprint of Octopus Publishing Group Ltd, Carmelite House, 50 Victoria Embankment, London EC4Y 0DZ
www.octopusbooks.co.uk

Distributed in the US by Hachette Book Group, 1290 Avenue of the Americas, 4th and 5th Floors, New York, NY 10104

Distributed in Canada by Canadian Manda Group, 664 Annette St., Toronto, Ontario, Canada M6S 2C8

Interior Styling: Lynda Gardener (except for pages 21, 33 top right, 39 middle right, 45 bottom left, 45 top right, 57 bottom centre, 65 middle left, 65 bottom right and 182–99 by Ali Heath; and page 27 top centre by Eleisha Gray.)

ISBN 978-1-78472-739-0

A CIP catalogue record for this book is available from the British Library.

Printed and bound in China

16

Book concept and text: Ali Heath
Creative Direction: Lynda Gardener and Ali Heath

Publisher: Alison Starling
Creative Director: Jonathan Christie
Editor: Faye Robson
Copy Editor: Zia Mattocks
Senior Production Manager: Katherine Hockley